From the Best Selling Author of *The Power of Serving Others*

Foreword by Jim Mitchum, CEO, Heart to Heart International

YOU'LL NEVER BE THE SAME

TRANSFORM YOUR LIFE BY SERVING OTHERS

GARY MORSCH *and* **STEVE WEBER**

www.dustjacket.com

DEDICATION

We dedicate this book to the many thousands of
Heart to Heart volunteers who have gone to the ends of
the earth to serve. As they addressed the greatest of need,
their lives were transformed in the process,
and they will never, ever, be the same!

This book is also dedicated to our wives,
Linda Weber (Steve) and Vickie Morsch (Gary),
who have lovingly stood by our sides as we followed
our calling to empower and enable others to serve.

And, to those who will read this book,
may you experience the transformational
power of serving others!

CONTENTS

FOREWORD

As I write this, only a few weeks into my new role as CEO of Heart to Heart International, I am looking down at the Atlantic Ocean from 33,000 feet. It's the same ocean that washes the white sand beaches of Southeastern Haiti where HHI has been engaged for the past five years to help rebuild a region devastated by an earthquake and victimized by poverty and disease. However, my destination is not Haiti this time. It's Liberia.

Ebola. Even the word conjures up fear as horrible images of this modern-day black plague are pasted all over cable, broadcast and online news outlets. As Liberia and West Africa descend into a deep, dark pool of humanitarian crisis without a visible bottom, no one, including me, wants to be there right now. And yet, that is exactly where I need to be.

Two weeks ago, Gary Morsch returned from leading our Advance Team into Liberia to determine the best way for HHI to help in this crisis beyond sending medical supplies. Our initial idea of providing medical assistance to some of the many thousands of Liberians with non-Ebola related health needs was scuttled when the team learned there was no safe way to treat anyone until Ebola is under control. To do otherwise was to condemn the clinician to become the next Ebola victim.

After much careful deliberation with the HHI Board, we decided that HHI should do what we have been asked to do by responsible authorities in Liberia, and open an Ebola Treatment Unit. I am now on my way to Liberia's capital, Monrovia, to help oversee preparations for the most complex, challenging, and dangerous mission we have ever undertaken.

When asked why HHI would go to Liberia in the midst of the largest Ebola outbreak ever known, I can only say it is because we must. People are dying. And our responsibility, our mission, is to help them. We know no greater purpose than to care for people in need. It is why Gary and the others started Heart to Heart International twenty-two years ago, and what our volunteers are once again stepping forward to do, despite the risks. Plus, we know that when we care for others, we transform our own lives for the better.

Perhaps the most compelling reason of all is found in the New Testament of the Bible. In Matthew 25:40 it says, "And the King will say, 'I tell you the truth, when you did it to one of the least of these my brothers and sisters, you were doing it to me.'"

Jim Mitchum
CEO, Heart to Heart International

INTRODUCTION *Part 1*

As you and I think back over our lives, we can no doubt identify a few people who have made a huge impact on us. Their words or actions or examples have made us into the people we are today, and sometimes have even turned our lives upside down.

Mother Teresa was one of those people in my life. I first met her when I was a volunteer. Soon after I started my medical practice, I decided that I would travel to Kolkata (formerly called Calcutta), India, to volunteer for the Sisters of Charity, as her Catholic order was known. Of course, what I really wanted was the opportunity to meet the famous nun who had started it all.

Not only did I meet Mother Teresa and volunteer with her Sisters, but she and I also became friends. Little did I know that this stooped, elderly nun would change my life. My friendship with Mother Teresa planted a seed in my heart and mind.

Those who were close to her simply called her "Mother." To Mother and her Sisters I was "Doctor." Though I didn't realize it at the time, her answers to my probing questions, along with my observations of "Mother in action," were laying the foundation for a global humanitarian organization that would someday touch the lives of millions.

The lessons I learned from Mother Teresa became the heart and soul of Heart to Heart International. They are the values that guide our volunteers today. They are the principles that you will read about in this book. If you put them into practice, your life will be transformed, as mine was.

This book is the third in a trilogy that Dr. Dean Nelson and I have co-authored, and it's really a continuation of our first two books, *Heart and Soul: Awakening Your Passion to Serve* (1997) and *The Power of Serving Others: You Can Start Where You Are* (2006). Dean and I are joined by a third author, Dr. Steve Weber. Steve is another person who has changed my life in a significant way. Many years ago I went to Haiti as a volunteer doctor. He was a missionary in Haiti at the time. Fast forward to today, and Steve Weber works for Heart to Heart, directing all our work in that country.

The message of this book is not new. Mother Teresa embodied it in Kolkata. Steve Weber embodied it in Haiti. Heart to Heart International has carried this message to more than 150 nations across the globe.

The message is simple:

*By dedicating some portion of your life
to serving others, you will discover an inner
power that will transform you.*

I experienced this firsthand through the life of Mother Teresa. Thousands of others have experienced it when they have volunteered with Heart to Heart International. I am confident you will experience this same message when you read this book.

Gary Morsch
Founder, Heart to Heart International

INTRODUCTION *Part 2*

My wife and I first arrived in Haiti during the mid 1970s. At that time Haiti was often referred to as "The Pearl of the Antilles." Such a reference reflected Haiti's natural beauty, not only of its people but also of the mountains that cover the island. I immediately fell head-over-heels in love with "The Pearl," and have dedicated decades there, despite it being a country that defies labeling.

Much has changed in Haiti since the mid 1970s. And, unfortunately, many of the changes have been for the worse. It is hard to find signs of significant progress. However, these pages will reveal examples I find exciting, one of which is a movement I call "from survival to sustainability."

I will always be grateful to my long-time friend, Dr. Gary Morsch, because he had the idea of asking Linda and me if we would consider coming out of retirement to give leadership to Heart to Heart's on-the-ground response to Haiti's January 12, 2010, devastating earthquake. The truth is, retirement *is* overrated. I have found much fulfillment since returning to my adopted country, more than words can adequately express.

I have enjoyed working on this book project with my old friend Gary, and my new friend Dean Nelson. What a great duo they are! They both are fun to work with and crazy full of life! I trust as you read this book you will find very significant take-a-ways as you follow the interesting pathways Heart to Heart has taken around the world. These activities are radically changing the lives of many wonderful people.

Steve Weber
Executive Director, Heart to Heart International – Haiti
Port-au-Prince

INTRODUCTION *Part 3*

ang around with Gary Morsch and Steve Weber for a while, and a couple of things will occur to you quickly. First, you'll discover that they are extraordinary people. For one thing, I don't think they sleep. I have been with them in different parts of the world, and they always are able to squeeze in one more conversation with a patient, a parishioner, a political leader, a co-worker or a perfect stranger. They can take one more phone call to solve a problem thousands of miles away, or in the next town. They exhaust me.

They also think bigger than most people. That doesn't mean they are dreamers who come up with useless ideas. They are dreamers who see problems *and* solutions. Pretty much every conversation with them will include one of them saying, "Why are we doing it that way?" That always means they have spotted an inefficiency, a system flaw. They instantly jump on ways to do things more effectively with better return on investment and effort. But they don't do it so they can make more money. They do it so that people can live better lives. They do it to save lives. They see ways to relieve suffering in the world. And they see ways to provide opportunities for people to live deeper, more meaningful lives. A lot of the world's problems would be solved if more people would listen to these two. They inspire me.

They are also impatient, but for all of the right reasons. When they see that something could save lives, who wouldn't want to change things for the better?

But even if they are impatient, they ALWAYS see the broader context. They are also realists, and they know that sometimes changing the big picture takes longer.

Gary and Steve asked me to get involved in this book, and they had an idea of what it should be about. But as is always the case with them, once we got to work, they realized that the theme was much bigger. This is the third book I have worked on with Gary. The first, *Heart and Soul: Awakening Your Passion to Serve,* was a call for people to realize that serving others was something that everyone can do, and that deep down, something that everyone wants to do. The second one, *The Power of Serving Others*, showed how serving others can transform your life and give it meaning. This one is a continuation of those themes, with new insights about what we are put on this earth to do. I spent many, many hours with Gary and Steve in Haiti as well as the U.S. putting their thoughts, passions and stories into the context of this book's message.

This book got much of its inspiration from people in some of the organizations that have come alongside Heart to Heart

International in Haiti and other parts of the world. Those groups include the Association of the Peasants of Fondwa and Father Joseph Philippe; the Sisters of Charity of Leavenworth, Kansas; the Church of the Nazarene in Haiti and Dr. Walliere Pierre; One Heart – Many Hands and George Sisler; Mid-America Nazarene University in Olathe, Kansas; the United Methodist Church of the Resurrection and Rev. Cayce Stapp; the American Jewish Joint Distribution Committee; the Federation of the Peasants of Pichon and Rev. Samerite Deruisseaux; Becton Dickinson (BD); and Bayada Home Health Care. Other groups that inspire us who have worked with Heart to Heart from the early years to the present are the American Academy of Family Physicians, Welch Allyn, Johnson and Johnson and FedEx.

Individuals have inspired us as well. Some have worked as volunteers with Heart to Heart, and some have just given great advice, assistance, counsel and friendship. They include Jadh Lyke, JD; Duane Spaulding, MD; Janice Ballard, MPH; Robis Pierre in the Ministry of Planning and External Cooperation, Government of Haiti; Delson Merisier, MD, in Leogane, Haiti; and Dylan Aebersold.

Franklin Cook, a friend to all three of us, and his assistant, Joanna Hamel, did a great deal of research and conducted dozens of interviews to make this book possible.

To all of the organizations and individuals listed, Steve, Gary and I are grateful for how they helped shape the ideas you're about to read. And to you, the reader, I think you'll get a sense of the boundless energy of Gary and Steve, which is motivated by their hearts of compassion and desire to serve others. I don't think this book will exhaust you. But I hope it inspires you.

Dean Nelson
San Diego, California

Chapter 1

DO THE RIGHT THING

A few days after the earthquake in Haiti, Gary walked into a United Nations tent that was being used as a field hospital, staffed by personnel from the University of Miami's hospitals and medical school. Hundreds of cots were lined up in rows, and every cot was filled with injured Haitians. Gary had seen things like this before in his work as a doctor in war zones. He had also seen similar scenarios when responding to disasters such as tornadoes, earthquakes and hurricanes in other parts of the world.

But nothing in his experience prepared him for the smell of that tent.

"It was the smell of death," he said, shaking his head slowly, as if trying to rid the odor from his memory. "It nearly knocked me off my feet."

The tent trapped the heat, insects and scent of post-earthquake Haiti. Gangrene had set into many of the victims, the result of the makeshift hospital treating contaminated wounds. Flies were impossible to keep out; moaning and howling was the white noise. A tarp hung in the back of the tent, and on the other side of it doctors amputated limbs in unsterile surroundings. In addition to the crying and screaming, Gary could occasionally hear a severed limb hit the ground.

"It was like being sent back in time to the U.S. Civil War," he said. "I couldn't believe what I was seeing, smelling and hearing."

The United States military had asked Gary to be on the lookout for U.S. citizens who needed to be evacuated. The head of the hospital told Gary about a critically ill patient who was an American. The patient was going to die if he wasn't evacuated very soon. Gary said he would contact the military on the patient's behalf.

Gary went to the command post and talked to the doctor in charge of medical evacuations. That doctor asked Gary if he could bring the patient to the airport. No, Gary said – the patient needed an ambulance. The doctor pondered Gary's information for a few moments, and then got up.

"Follow me," he said.

He flagged down a military vehicle. At a checkpoint they picked up a state department official and drove to the makeshift hospital.

Many Haitians have dual citizenship with the United States, and many more are U.S. citizens but frequently visit their home country. This man was visiting when the earthquake struck. He was rescued from underneath rubble, and his injuries had caused great loss of blood and already the loss of one limb.

Gary knew that one of the U.S. government's priorities in the first few days after the earthquake was to evacuate its citizens, regardless of the cost or circumstances.

"How can you know for sure that he's an American citizen?" Gary asked.

"It's not an exact science, but we can ask some questions," the state department official said.

At the hospital, a nurse pointed out the man.

He was weak and dehydrated. The stump from his amputated leg had turned black with gangrene. He was in shock, and Gary knew he was close to death. Flies crawled across the man's face, but he was too weak to wave them away. His lips were dry and cracked.

Gary and the state department official introduced themselves to the patient. The moaning of the other patients stopped as they observed the exchange.

"Sir, what is your name?" the official asked.

The man could barely get out his name.

"Sir, do you have a U.S. passport with you?"

The man said it was back in his house, which was destroyed.

"Sir, where were you born?"

The man replied.

"Sir, what is your date of birth?"

The man was getting weaker.

Come on! Gary thought. *He's not going to live long enough to answer all these questions!*

The man gave his date of birth.

"Sir, what is your Social Security number?"

The official had told Gary that if the man could answer this one question, he would accept the man's answer as proof of his citizenship. Gary was pulling for the man. The man's life depended on answering this one question.

Gary thought, *God, help him remember that number.*

The man slowly gave his nine-digit number.

"Yes!" Gary whispered to himself.

"Sir, welcome to the United States of America," the official declared.

When it was clear that this man was going to be evacuated and his life saved, the other victims in the tent erupted in cheers.

Hearing this story, Steve, a resident of Haiti for decades, was not surprised.

"It is very consistent with Haitian culture to cheer when someone can leave," said Steve. "Some assume *they* have no future here, but if they see someone getting out, well, they're happy for that person."

Gary and the official picked up the man's cot and carried it outside to the military truck, while those who were going to be left behind clapped and whistled. Then the truck headed for the airport. The official radioed ahead to get a medical evacuation plane ready, and when they arrived, a giant Air Force cargo plane was already waiting, cleared for takeoff, with the engines running. The plane, which usually was loaded down with tons of equipment and hundreds of troops, was empty except for about 10 medical personnel aboard, ready to give their full attention to this one Haitian-American survivor en route to a hospital in Florida.

It worked out well for that one person in that makeshift hospital tent.

But something about it didn't sit well with Gary. He didn't have a lot of time to reflect on the incident until a few days later. The conclusions he came to troubled him.

In a hospital tent with hundreds of dying people, one person got adequate medical care. And not just adequate medical care – a crew of medical personnel and a cargo plane that was otherwise empty, was dedicated specifically to that one person. Gary couldn't even begin to calculate the cost of that patient's medical evacuation and care.

He was happy that the odds of the man surviving had increased significantly. Gary was even impressed with the efficiency and commitment that the U.S. had for taking care of its own. But It didn't seem right that this person, who didn't choose where he was born, received some of the best medical care in the world, and the others in the tent, who also didn't choose where they were born, were left behind to suffer, many of whom would die.

"We can't just walk away from these people," he thought. "We can't just take care of our own."

Putting his head together with Steve, Gary knew that they weren't going to solve Haiti's healthcare system problems. But they knew they could do *something*. They knew they could start *somewhere*.

"I gave an order as a military doctor and a life was saved," Gary said. "I wondered how many more lives we could save?"

LESSONS FROM CHINA

It was this kind of thinking that developed into a long-term relationship between Heart to Heart and China back in the 1990s, when Heart to Heart conducted an airlift of medical supplies and distributed them to communities in hard-to-reach areas in the Sichuan Province.

Since then, the Chinese government has asked Heart to Heart to help improve major aspects of the country's health care system. The government told Heart to Heart that there were more than 600 million people living in poverty who did not have access to adequate health care.

"We tried to ask the Chinese medical people what they needed, but it was hard to get them to open up at first," Gary said. "They weren't ready to talk about it."

So Heart to Heart brought in medical supplies, distributed them and did it again each year for a few years. After a few of these medical airlifts, a member of the Sichuan Health Ministry said to some of the volunteer Heart to Heart doctors, "Tell us about how you were trained." The ministry official confessed that the region had one of the highest infant mortality rates in the country, and asked for suggestions in how to improve medical care for babies. In a culture that did not readily admit to weaknesses, Gary knew that this was a new level of relationship between the health ministry and Heart to Heart.

Gary remembers walking into a labor-and-delivery room in a hospital during one of his first visits to China and asking if they had a laryngoscope, the instrument used to resuscitate infants. The doctor opened a drawer and pulled one out. It was not sterilized, but lying freely in the drawer. It had dried blood on it and the light at the end didn't work. Gary felt that this was an indication of how deeply the region needed help in taking care of infants.

In those initial visits into China, Heart to Heart staffers were naturally viewed with some suspicion. The relationship was cordial on the surface, but the volunteers' movements were constantly monitored. When two countries have the level of mistrust that once existed between the United States and China, just because a group calls itself humanitarian doesn't mean it's really a humanitarian group. But that suspicion didn't last long.

Heart to Heart and the ministry of health jointly developed a course, called "First Breath," in neo-natal resuscitation techniques to teach doctors and nurses who would then train their counterparts. The goal was to train the trainers, which is a core value of Heart to Heart's, and the result was that thousands of doctors and nurses were and continue to be trained in this practice. This has saved tens of thousands of lives. The training was so valuable and successful that the ministry now mandates that every nurse and doctor who takes care of newborns be certified in this training. The program was adopted throughout the Sichuan Province and has expanded into the Tibetan Autonomous Region. The area had one of the highest infant mortality rates in the country, and now it has one of the lowest.

A few years after First Breath's success, Heart to Heart asked the health ministry what else the province needed. The ministry told them that high in the mountains of Sichuan, a large percentage of people suffered from cataracts. The afflicted were mostly farmers who spent much of their days outside, under intense sun at a high altitude. Their blindness created great hardship on the families, and health care was more than a day's walk over rugged terrain. If they couldn't see, then the farmers couldn't work. Heart to Heart brought in an ophthalmology program in partnership with the Dean McGee Eye Institute of Oklahoma. Called "Fresh Vision," the program provides training to Chinese ophthalmologists in how to perform cataract surgery in rural areas. Through a mobile eye training unit, volunteer ophthalmologists could now go to the villages to train local doctors in cataract surgery instead of waiting for patients to be brought to the city. Within the first few years, newly trained Chinese doctors performed more than 100,000 cataract operations in the region.

Jon North, the former CEO of Heart to Heart, remembers going with the mobile eye treatment unit to a hard-to-reach community, and meeting the wife of a farmer who was inside the clinic having his cataracts removed.

"She told me what life was like once her husband went blind and couldn't work," he said. "She had to walk eight hours to her job, and had to leave her husband and her parents behind for several days at a time. She grabbed me and thanked me for allowing her husband to see, so that she could now take proper care of her parents and provide her family dignity. It's encounters like those that mean everything. My friend, Dr. Brad, was in that clinic giving sight to the blind. This family, and thousands of others, had their lives made right again."

A frequent question Chinese medical workers ask Heart to Heart volunteers is how much they are being paid to come to China to do this training. When the volunteers say that, not only are they not being paid, but that they also are using vacation time from their jobs at home, and that they paid their own way, including plane fare, meals, and accommodations, the workers repeatedly ask, "Why do you do this? Why do you come so far to donate your time to help strangers?"

The answer from the volunteers is always the same.

"It's the right thing to do," they say.

This has been Gary's drumbeat since Heart to Heart began. The agency is more than pills or product or airlifts or training. The goal is to light a spark of compassion that will grow throughout the world, until millions of people in every nation will give of themselves in service to others.

A Chinese health official took Gary aside one day and told him very cautiously that he agreed with Gary in how the world could be changed for the better. He talked about how governments often do exactly the wrong thing when they want to influence others. When a person or a nation uses power and might to get their way, the official said, it creates hatred and a desire for revenge among the vanquished. His own country had done this, and he told Gary that some believe that the U.S. did this in Iraq. "You are creating new enemies that will not forget what happened to them," he said. Then the man paused. "America should have sent in an army of volunteers from Heart to Heart to Iraq," he said. "That is how you would have created long-term good for that country!"

Given the irony of being exhorted by a Chinese government official about a country abusing its power, Gary could only smile. Deep down, though, Gary agreed with the analysis.

Gary also knew that the official was aware of the irony. The official knew that, after being in the Sichuan Province, Heart to Heart was next headed for Tibet to do training with that region's medical personnel. China's relationship with Tibet has been a source of animosity and violence between the two regions for generations. It was Heart to Heart's way to tell their hosts in China that serving others went beyond racial, geographic and historical boundaries. Serving others means going where there is need, not just where your political allies are.

More than ten years after first being invited to help train doctors and nurses in China, Heart to Heart was asked to get more deeply involved in how the Sichuan Province actually *delivered* health care. This time it involved a system for training family physicians. China's central government had told each province that they needed to establish a network of community health centers staffed by family physicians. This was a departure from the specialist model the country had worked from for decades. And since Sichuan had a thriving relationship with Heart to Heart, the provincial leaders turned to the organization again.

As they have done wherever they have worked in the world, Heart to Heart asked one simple question of the Sichuan Ministry of Health, in regard to family medicine: What do you need? The answer was simple – "Help us train the trainers of family physicians."

Training trainers is what Heart to Heart knew how to do.

"We were practically pinching ourselves after they told us this," said Gary. "Training the trainers is at the heart of our programs. It's what we'd been doing in China for more than a decade – in neonatal resuscitation, ophthalmology and emergency medicine. Now they were inviting us to partner with them in training the pioneer family medicine educators that will lead to massive improvements in health care in China."

Heart to Heart invited a team of Chinese health care leaders to visit the U.S. and arranged meetings with family medicine leaders, medical schools and family medicine residencies. Most of this was done through a partnership with the American Osteopathic Association (AOA). Several groups from the AOA also conducted training seminars in the province, in conjunction with one of the largest hospitals and medical schools in the world, called Hua Xi. The hospital was started in 1892 by Christian missionaries, and now it is the leading hospital and health care training center for all of western China, which represents the majority of the country's population. Those missionaries did what they thought was the right thing more than 100 years ago.

An additional program between Heart to Heart and the province was an ongoing training of emergency workers and first responders. That training was put into practice in 2008, when an 8.0 earthquake rocked the area. Approximately 70,000 people were killed, 375,000 were injured, and another 20,000 were never found. About 80 percent of the region's buildings were destroyed. Estimates were that between 5 million and 11 million people were homeless as a result. The epicenter was about 50 miles from the provincial capital of Chengdu, where Heart to Heart's office is, and the shock was felt a thousand miles away.

Dr. Brian Robinson, Heart to Heart's medical director in Chengdu, was seen on Chinese television shaking hands with China's Premier Wen Jiabao in the middle of the earthquake zone.

Because of Heart to Heart's reputation in the region, their Chengdu office was inundated with people volunteering to help. Some were Chinese residents, some were Americans living in the area who had been teaching English or doing business there, and others were from other world regions. More than 5,000 volunteers showed up at Heart to Heart's offices, or were directed there by other agencies, asking how they could help. They were organized into three types of teams, depending on people's skill level. Day Teams were made up of 8-10 people who traveled to various areas to distribute food, water, bedding and other supplies. Thirty-Six Hour Teams did the same thing, but went farther out and spent the night in the field. Extreme Teams consisted of healthy backpackers who hiked into the mountains carrying water purification systems, medicines and other supplies, and were out for several days at a time.

Just in the previous year, Heart to Heart had done disaster training with the province's emergency responders.

In addition to mobilizing volunteers, Heart to Heart is known for donating millions of dollars of pharmaceuticals and medical supplies around the world. Those supplies are donated by some of the largest medical companies such as Johnson and Johnson, Sanofi Aventis, Pfizer, Teva, Cardinal Health and BD

(Becton, Dickinson and Company). FedEx, a long-time partner with Heart to Heart, has provided aircraft to transport these supplies. Once again, FedEx provided a cargo plane, which was filled with millions of dollars' worth of donated product, to Chengdu, China.

A RADICAL NOTION

Jeff Alpert, a doctor from western Kansas who volunteered with Heart to Heart after the earthquake in China, was one of the first doctors to respond two years later when the earthquake hit Haiti. The Heart to Heart office asked him how soon he could get to Miami. Alpert, like all of the volunteers, paid his own way to Haiti, and used his vacation days. He started seeing patients the day he arrived, working in the soccer stadium where much of the earthquake triage was centered. He was there for twelve days. He treated people with fractures, infected wounds, tetanus, cholera, shock, and countless other conditions. He has returned to the country six times since the earthquake, working mostly in the mountain clinics established by Heart to Heart, alongside Haitian doctors and nurses, seeing about sixty patients per day.

"It's not like Haiti is halfway around the world," he said. "I have the skills. How can you *not* do this? It's the right thing to do."

GARY MORSCH and STEVE WEBER

Doing the right thing isn't always easy. Sometimes you're misunderstood. One of Heart to Heart's strongest supporters is former U.S. Senator Robert Dole of Kansas. Dole was responsible for getting the first Air Force C-5 cargo plane for Heart to Heart's airlift to Russia in 1992. But when it became clear that Heart to Heart was shipping pediatric medicines to North Korea in the 1990s, Dole questioned Gary about the wisdom of aiding an enemy. North Korea? Gary listened to the senator, and then explained that the method he was using to get medicines into North Korea ensured that they would not go to the government or the military, but to the children. North Korean children were not our enemy, Gary maintained, they were victims of a tyrannical government. When Gary was done explaining, Senator Dole understood.

Whenever Gary speaks to groups, he often quotes the Sermon on the Mount, where Jesus tells us to love our enemies.

"One of the most powerful ideas in the world is this radical notion of loving our enemies," he said. "One small act of generosity to enemies can do far more than any weapon."

Heart to Heart does have a list of enemies. They include "lack of health care," "lack of access to clean water," "hunger," among others. But they don't include people. This explains why the organization's record of service includes many who have been considered enemies by some.

It also includes the people of Vietnam after the war, even when there were no diplomatic relations between the United States and Vietnam.

Heart to Heart put together an airlift of medical supplies to Vietnam in 1995, because the country was suffering greatly from the lack of adequate medical care. The longer version of this story appears in the book *Heart and Soul: Awakening Your Passion to Serve.* Gary went to several civic and veterans groups to get support for this airlift. He was met with more than a little skepticism. Weren't the Vietnamese our enemy? Didn't their soldiers torture our soldiers? And besides, who would fly the supplies into the country? No airline would risk its reputation to violate the U.S. State Department's embargo on commercial traffic into that region.

Except for FedEx. Bob Lewis, a former U.S. Marine and a Vietnam War veteran, saw Gary's vision for serving suffering people – especially those we once considered our enemy. Lewis contacted his platoon buddy, "Freddy" Smith, the CEO of FedEx. Smith called Lewis and asked for more details. They worked out permissions from the State Department, and that FedEx cargo plane, loaded with millions of dollars of life-saving medicines, was the first nonmilitary aircraft to land in Hanoi since the end of the war. The FedEx pilots who volunteered to fly that mission had previously flown bombing missions over Vietnam. They saw that flying in "weapons of mass salvation," a term humanitarian Paul Farmer uses for widely needed medicine, was better than dropping weapons of destruction.

It was the right thing to do. Even though the U.S. had placed an embargo on Vietnam, Heart to Heart believed that a bridge of goodwill needed to be built between the people of Vietnam and the United States. The embargo was creating great economic hardship that was mostly punishing the citizens, especially the most vulnerable, Gary felt. His hope was that this would be a step toward removing the embargo.

Through patient dialogue between Heart to Heart representatives and the Vietnamese government, approvals were finally granted. The airlift was a success, and the embargo was soon dropped. Many attribute this historic airlift in helping re-establish diplomatic relations with that country.

"Never underestimate the power of generosity, even to our former enemies," Gary said.

The Vietnamese have a national museum that presents a history of their war with the U.S. Following the Heart to Heart airlift, the government added an exhibit. The very last display includes photos of unloading the FedEx plane. It marked the true end of the war, according to the museum.

"We did the right thing," Gary said.

Sometimes personal pride can get in the way of doing the right thing. But when you see the bigger picture, pride can look pretty petty. That's one of the things Gary learned in Leogane, Haiti, when he discovered the perfect place to establish Heart to Heart's medical operation in that part of the country. Leogane had a hospital, but the building had mostly collapsed. Gary visited the area, and the hospital administrator came out of the rubble to greet him. Gary identified himself and said he was looking for a place to set up a triage and treatment center. The grounds surrounding the hospital looked perfect. It was one of the few shaded, cool locations in the entire region. The administrator agreed, and they shook hands on the deal.

Just then, a jeep pulled up with a representative from the large international organization Médecins Sans Frontières (MSF, or Doctors Without Borders). He announced to the administrator that the area would be perfect for them to set up a full field hospital and wanted permission to get started immediately. The administrator looked perplexed – what should he do? But Gary intervened.

"You're right – this would be perfect for you," Gary said. "We'll find another location."

Disappointed, Gary ended up in a sun-scorched soccer field in the heart of what once was downtown Leogane. But there was an up-side to this location. It was in that place where Heart to Heart met a group of Mennonites who had a mission in Leogane. Their compound had sustained only minor damage, and they offered to feed and house all of the staff and volunteers. For many months after the earthquake, hundreds of volunteers slept in tents on the Mennonite mission grounds and were served some of the best home-cooked meals imaginable.

In a speech to the University of Miami medical school, Paul Farmer concluded by telling the graduates that they will be tempted to give up their medical practice because they will ultimately be overwhelmed by all the suffering in the world. The speech was reprinted in the book *To Repair The World*. Doing the right thing will seem pointless against the sheer magnitude of the need, he said. He then referred to *The Two Towers*, the second movie in *The Lord of the Rings* trilogy, and dialogue between Sam and Frodo.

"Folks in those stories had a lot of chances of turning back, only they didn't. They were holding on to something," said Sam.

"What are we holding on to, Sam?" asks Frodo.

"That there's some good in this world, and it's worth fighting for," he said.[1]

Serving others – even if they're our enemies or when the odds are against us – is simply the right thing to do.

YOU'LL NEVER BE THE SAME

Chapter 2

COME ALONGSIDE

The Sisters in Kansas were panicking. They were part of a Catholic order headquartered in Leavenworth, and they were trying to reach their Sisters in Haiti who had been in partnership with them since the 1990s. The 2010 earthquake had disrupted cell phone and Internet connections.

The Haitian nuns were in a mountain community called Fondwa, an extremely remote location, accessible by roads that challenged even the most rugged vehicles. One side of the road might be mountain, and the other side might be cliff. To accommodate the mountain, the switchbacks were made passable by only horse or motorcycle. A more formal road was installed in the 1980s, but even that made veteran truck drivers stop in their tracks.

And yet tens of thousands of people lived in or around Fondwa. For generations they lived there with no local health care or schools. Father Joseph Philippe is a priest who grew up in Fondwa. He said that no one seemed to question the fact that a person needed to walk for more than one hour just to get clean water. "It was normal for us," he said.

Father Joseph had left Fondwa to further his education at Catholic Theological Union Seminary in Chicago, returning in 1988. While away from Haiti he developed a vision for the community. When he came back, he established a school, an agricultural program, a credit union, an orphanage, a house for the Sisters, and a university. The nuns' ministry spread to other parts of Haiti, and Father Joseph was widely seen as a visionary who could help develop a new kind of Haiti. He was Haitian, using Haitian people, to improve Haiti.

"For years I saw Haiti in a cycle of dependency on other governments and nonprofit groups," he said. "They rarely asked us what we wanted or needed. They often initiated programs or systems that didn't work here. Then, after the money was gone, what was left? I knew we had to break that cycle of dependency."

He knew that the way outside groups treated Haiti wasn't sustainable. It never is when someone else thinks they know what you need.

Father Joseph knew that if he could get the Haitian people organized so that they could better articulate what they actually needed, then Haiti could be less dependent on outside organizations and would have true ownership in determining its own future. If Haitians were coming up with solutions to their own problems, Father Joseph knew that those solutions would last. His efforts developed into an organization called the Association of Peasants of Fondwa (APF), and the members became voices to articulate what their communities' biggest needs were. The focus of APF was on schools and health care at the community level. APF became so influential that the national government developed a branch that concentrated specifically on what was called Peasant Affairs.

On that fateful day in January 2010, Father Joseph was in Port-au-Prince, a three-hour drive from Fondwa. The building he was in shook violently, and other buildings nearby collapsed. It felt like the end of the world.

"I gave what I thought was my final prayer – 'God, my life is in your hands,'" he said. He thought about Fondwa and wondered about the safety of the people there. Hours later, when he finally got access to a phone, he couldn't reach anyone. He knew that was a bad sign.

What he didn't yet know was that Fondwa was virtually at the epicenter of the earthquake. The orphanage had collapsed, killing some of the children. The Sisters' house also fell, killing two of the nuns. The school walls caved in, killing two maintenance workers. Twenty-three people in that community were killed. Not a single building survived.

There was no electricity, water, food, cell phone signal or access. As the Sisters huddled on the top of the mountain in Fondwa, they wondered how long it would take to be rescued. Would anyone remember us? Who would know if any of us survived? And where was Father Joseph? Was he even alive?

Back in Kansas, the Sisters of Charity in Leavenworth were asking the same questions. Unable to make direct contact with the Sisters in Fondwa, the only information they had was from news coverage of the earthquake. When the epicenter was finally pinpointed, they were filled with dread. It was Leogone, the closest city to Fondwa, and the entire region had suffered great losses, according to the reports. They feared the worst.

Gary didn't know about any of this. He'd never met the Sisters in Leavenworth or Fondwa. He was about to get on a private plane headed for Haiti, and was trying to arrange a place to stay once he got in that country. Lou Ann Hummel, a staffer in one of Gary's companies called Docs Who Care, had worked with the Sisters of Charity in Leavenworth and remembered their connection to the Sisters in Fondwa. She called Leavenworth to see if they knew of a place where Gary could stay.

Some of the Fondwa Sisters happened to be in Leavenworth at the time. When they heard that Gary was going to Haiti, they asked if he could check on their community. Lou Ann relayed the request to Gary, and he said he'd try, even though he had never heard of Fondwa, and didn't know where it was. Then he continued trying to arrange a place to stay.

When he finally got into *Port-au-Prince*, he went to the central location where many of the injured and dying had been taken, which was the soccer stadium. It was like walking onto the set of a movie about the apocalypse. Hundreds of tents provided shade from the searing sun for survivors. Medical workers treated gashes, infections, broken bones, and crushed limbs in this makeshift trauma center. Every part of the world was represented by volunteers who had dropped everything and rushed in to address the immediate needs of those suffering from the earthquake damage. Water stations, latrines and food tables were also throughout the stadium.

Gary began treating the injured and coordinating Heart to Heart's medical team, but as a colonel in the U.S. Army Reserve, he was also able to procure vehicles and supplies when he became aware of needs elsewhere. He was constantly on the move, directing supplies to specific regions, and directing medical staff to where the needs were greatest.

A few days after he arrived in Haiti, he remembered the request to check on the Sisters of Fondwa. Then he found out where it was and how hard it would be to get there.

"Ninety-nine times out of 100 in a case like that, I would have to say no," Gary said later. "The roads were impossible because of rock slides. There were no available vehicles, and, frankly, we didn't have time. People were dying right in front of us. How could I drive out into the mountains looking for a village that I've never heard of?"

But he hired a driver and a four-wheel drive vehicle and, with Heart to Heart staff and supplies, he headed into the mountains toward Leogone, and then took the narrow rocky path to Fondwa. What he saw nearly took his breath away.

He looked from one collapsed building to another. Finally, he saw the Sisters huddled under a shade tree, comforting some of the children. They had no food or water. Some were injured; two Sisters had been killed, and there were no doctors or nurses. No one even knew they were there. Gary and his staff were the first outsiders to arrive.

"It was a scene from hell," Gary said. "It was just such chaos. We had food, water and medicine and gave away everything we had."

Gary and the others sat with the Sisters under the tree and found out what had happened and what they needed. They had already buried their dead. Gary used his satellite phone to put the Sisters from Fondwa in touch with the Sisters in Leavenworth. He looked at the rubble that used to be classrooms and dwellings. He knew he was departing from the normal Heart to Heart response when he promised the Sisters, "We will help you rebuild this community."

Heart to Heart's typical response to disaster is to provide emergency medical assistance anywhere in the world, and then, when the situation stabilizes, to leave. In this moment Gary knew he was taking a different path.

"I don't know why I made this promise, but it seemed right," he said. "I knew we were going to be here for a long time."

Gary got the Canadian military to bulldoze and blast the boulders from the road. Heart to Heart staffers soon connected with Father Joseph.

"It took me a few days to realize that everything was gone," Father Joseph said. "But we're not the first people to experience bad things. The Bible is full of stories of people who suffered from terrible events. It is humanity's story."

Since he had already been through the process of establishing an orphanage, school and shelter once before, Father Joseph had an idea of what he needed to do. He knew he was going to need outside help. But he also didn't want to lapse into that cycle of dependency on other organizations. He didn't want their strings attached. He wanted for Fondwa what Fondwa needed, not what some outside group thought they needed.

"Gary is a good listener," he said, recalling his first meeting with Heart to Heart. "I talked to him about doing more than emergency relief and asked if he'd participate with me in doing something long-term."

BROADER VISION

This was a type of paradigm shift for Gary. He knew what to do in the soccer stadium in Port-au-Prince, which was to relieve the suffering of those who needed immediate assistance. His method was the same as most other medical relief agencies: See as many patients as possible in as little time as possible.

He had done this with the tsunami in 2004, after Hurricane Katrina in New Orleans in 2005, in Chengdu, China, after its earthquake in 2008, after countless disasters caused by weather, political corruption, or war in countless regions around the world.

He knew what to do in combat hospitals and military bases as a U.S. Army Reserve doctor in Iraq, Kuwait, Kosovo and Germany, treating soldiers and civilians wounded by bullets, roadside bombs, and aerial strikes. Stop the bleeding. Start the IV. Set the fractured bone. Prevent shock. Sew up the laceration. Send them back to the field or medevac them to larger hospitals. He knew how to relieve suffering on a short-term basis. Long term? That took a different kind of thinking. It was a different way to serve others. It meant investing time and resources in slow-moving processes. It meant commitment. And Father Joseph was the catalyst for that new kind of thinking.

This kind of paradigm shift is also what's sometimes necessary when we serve people around us in our families and communities. If a neighbor's house burns down, neighbors and social service agencies are often quick and efficient in responding to short-term needs like shelter, food, diapers, clothing, and transportation. Collections are taken to cover immediate expenses. Friends, church members and other volunteers help clean up. That's what a community does for its members. But after the immediate needs are met, what happens next? This is where sensitivity enters the picture, where we say to one another, "What do you need?"

What if the need is education or schools, basic sanitation or health, hunger, improving agricultural yields, erosion control? Those are longer-term involvements that are crucial, but are present well after the immediate crisis is over. We don't know what those needs are unless we ask. When we do, we are no longer relief workers. We're fellow human beings, on equal footing, not in a superior/inferior relationship.

But that kind of involvement and commitment is time consuming, risky, expensive, and may not have the desired outcomes. And what's true for a community is also true for a country.

"A lot of people say they want to help Haiti, but they really just help themselves," Father Joseph said. "I am very suspicious and critical of groups coming here to help us. I think Haitians should rebuild Haiti. But I'm realistic enough to know that we can't do it all by ourselves. We need outside support, people who will come alongside us."

Father Joseph, who always thinks long term, saw potential in a partnership with Heart to Heart. But seeing potential was not something new to this priest. He had lots of practice from his years of service in Fondwa. One of the young men in his community, Christophe Rodrigue, showed great promise as a leader and thinker, so Father Joseph invested in him with the scarce parish resources. In the 1990s he paid for Christophe's education in France, knowing that the risk was for Christophe to see how big and enticing the world was, and how bleak his future might be if he returned to Haiti.

Christophe completed his graduate studies, and then did indeed fly home from Paris. Father Joseph has invested similarly in more than fifty others from Fondwa. Wherever they trained in the world, all have returned, ready to serve. Investing even more deeply in Fondwa's future, Father Joseph suggested that Christophe work for Heart to Heart in Haiti. It was a perfect fit.

When Father Joseph started developing the orphanage, convent and school in Fondwa, he knew what was needed because he was from that area and was a leader in the community. He was in relationship with the people of that community. He knew what the long-term needs were.

"It was shocking to realize that all I had done for more than twenty years was gone," he said. "We were back to where we started."

The good news, though, was that now he knew what was possible.

"Before the 1980s, people accepted not having access to water," he said. "My mother and sister would walk more than an hour to get water. That was normal. So after the earthquake we knew what was possible and set our hearts to rebuilding our community. We knew that if we waited for the government to do it, it would never happen. The most important thing for us was to keep our hope alive."

One of the ways their hope was kept alive was through their relationship with Heart to Heart.

A few weeks after Gary's initial visit to Fondwa, he returned to the community with Steve Weber. This was Steve's first visit back to Haiti since he had worked there more than twenty years before as a missionary. They found Father Joseph in a small, white canvas tent protecting him from the sun. Inside the tent was a cot, a makeshift desk and stool, a car battery on the ground with wires leading to a laptop computer, where the priest was rapidly typing.

Gary introduced Father Joseph to Steve, and because of Steve's previous years in Haiti, they discovered that they had many friends in common. They also had similar interests in areas such as micro lending, construction, education and community development.

This is a match made in heaven, Gary recalls thinking at the time. "I knew in that moment that Steve was not leaving Haiti."

Steve and Gary asked the crucial question that those who serve others sometimes forget to ask: What do you need? What are you trying to accomplish? How can we help? Father Joseph said that Fondwa needed to rebuild the school, orphanage and Sisters' house. He had already lined up an architect. Oh yes – and they also needed a medical clinic.

Gary knew of a group in Wichita, Kansas, called Hospitals of Hope, that converted sea-going shipping containers into medical clinics. The containers were forty feet long, divided into three rooms, with air conditioning, a generator, lights and a water system. He committed to bringing a "Clinic In a Can" to Fondwa, and to staffing it with nurses every day and doctors once a week.

Steve committed to help rebuild the community.

SOMETHING BIG

By the end of their meeting with Father Joseph, something began to dawn on both Gary and Steve.

"There aren't too many days when I recognize that something big is happening right now," Gary said. "That time together was transcendent, as if we were all experiencing something supernatural. Some would call it a Divine Appointment. We knew that we'd be doing something of significance together."

This Divine Appointment is consistent with Father Joseph's view of why we are put on this earth.

"The most glory that one can give to God is to help other human beings to help themselves in living a decent life as God's daughters and sons," he said. "Every human being deserves to live in dignity, with schools and churches to attend, food and clean water for themselves and their children, access to health care and shelter, safe communities. I try to empower the poor, the young people, the women and the peasants. I want to see an improvement in their living conditions. I want to enable them to help themselves in a way that they can also help others. Life is a gift that we have received, and the best way to accept this gift is to share it with others as much as possible."

Within a few months, the medical clinic in a container arrived in Port-au-Prince. It was loaded on a truck at the port and began the long, treacherous journey through Leogane and then on the one-lane road to Fondwa. The rutted, uneven, lane took its toll, though. Each switchback increased in severity, until finally the driver stopped. Another turn and he felt that the container could tip the truck over the cliff. This was as far as he could go.

Near the road was a flat space where a family had built a shelter out of available scraps of metal, wood and cardboard. It was the only place in the area where the container would fit. Father Joseph walked up the path to the family's home and talked to them for a few minutes. Then he returned to the truck and the workers.

"We can put the clinic where that house is," he said calmly. The Heart to Heart staff was doubtful.

"What did you say to that family?" they asked.

"I told them we needed the area for a medical clinic for Fondwa, and they were happy to make room for it," he said.

The neighbor later recalled, "Father Joseph said he needed this space, so I said okay."

The Clinic In A Can now serves thousands from Fondwa and other communities higher in the mountains, where there had previously been no health care.

To address the school that had been destroyed in Fondwa, Heart to Heart met with the American Jewish Joint Distribution Committee (JDC). Heart to Heart and the JDC had worked together on other projects throughout the world. The JDC agreed to help fund the school and other facilities. The U.S. military provided fuel for bulldozers and other heavy equipment, and even loaned the community a construction block cutting machine. Those favors were a result of Gary's helping the military find runway space near Leogane for supply aircraft to take off and land. The people doing the actual construction were Haitians from that area.

Father Joseph is convinced that the process of rebuilding Fondwa is an example of how people can serve others while still being respectful, so that those being served can retain their dignity as human beings. It takes more time when we ask our neighbors what they need, and when we involve them as participants. But it's when we ask that we provide something that will last.

For Heart to Heart, getting involved in the rebuilding of Fondwa was not just about replacing buildings. They spent considerable time with Father Joseph, trying to discern what the people of Fondwa wanted, and what Heart to Heart could reasonably do. They didn't want to do anything *to* the people of Fondwa. They wanted to do something *with* them that would remain long-term.

For Father Joseph also, the goal was not just to replace buildings that had collapsed in Fondwa in the shortest amount of time. The goal was to know what the community needed in the aftermath of the earthquake, build the community better than it was before, using the people of Fondwa to improve their own situation.

"We are blessed to participate with Heart to Heart," he said. "It feels like there is now a concrete bridge between us."

Something about his experience in Haiti changed Gary's thinking. In his first visit immediately after the earthquake, he spent about a month in Haiti. The hospitals in Port-au-Prince were overwhelmed. The country had collapsed in both physical and figurative ways. Outlying mountain communities like Fondwa, which never had adequate health care even before the earthquake, were in even more dire need for health care, clean water, sanitation, and food. The longer he stayed and the more he saw, the more he realized that emergency measures were only part of the solution to what he was witnessing.

Sometimes the needs are bigger than splints, bandages and sutures. Sometimes the needs require us to stay awhile.

"I knew I couldn't solve all of the problems in Haiti," Gary said. "But I also knew that I couldn't just do emergency medicine and move on. For some reason, what I saw pulled me in further and called me to participate at a deeper level. I wasn't used to that."

In Port-au-Prince, it became clear that the soccer stadium could not be the long-term site for providing medical care to the earthquake victims. But health care was one of the biggest needs in the area. An ongoing plan needed to be developed. The timing of Wallière Pierre's visit to Gary in the stadium could not have been more perfect. Pierre was the pastor of a Nazarene church in Belaire, a community of Port-au-Prince that was once thriving and beautiful. It had descended into chaos in recent years, much like the rest of the city, and the area was full of gangs and violence. Pierre wanted his church to be a place of service to the community, but people were afraid to go there. Pierre showed Gary the neighborhood. The massive Catholic cathedral nearby had collapsed. Entire neighborhoods were leveled. They saw a man with one leg trying to walk.

In Gary's view, it was perfect. Heart to Heart moved its temporary medical operation from the soccer stadium and established a permanent medical clinic in the church. This transition included participation from the JDC, along with some of the largest health care companies in the world, including BD and Welch Allyn.

"Heart to Heart was the only organization that stayed," Pierre said. "Belaire is an area that is considered a red zone, and no NGO wanted to stay there. But people respect the authority of the church. The presence of Heart to Heart helps enforce and strengthen this authority. They offered services the church didn't have."

Heart to Heart didn't limit its involvement to medical care. They also sponsored neighborhood soccer teams and tournaments, provided wheelbarrows and shovels, so that local residents could clean up their own streets, and provided job training. The doctors and nurses working in the Belaire clinic are Haitian.

"People in the area could see that this church was helping them in their lives socially, spiritually and economically," said Pierre.

Within a few weeks of the earthquake, Gary could see that Heart to Heart could be part of Haiti's future. He began looking for a house to rent as a headquarters. He didn't have a plan for the long term, but he knew that this time Heart to Heart was going to stay a while.

YOU'LL NEVER BE THE SAME

Chapter 3

TAKE OUT THE TRASH

O f all of the stories Gary tells about his visits with Mother Teresa, audiences love this one the best.

The first time he met her he was a young doctor traveling the world. He arranged a visit with her and when he saw how few medicines she had access to for those who were dying and destitute, he promised to bring medicine to her sometime in the future. When he did, several years later, Heart to Heart brought 50 tons of medicine valued at more than $12 million, all donated by pharmaceutical companies. He also brought 90 volunteers. He knew Mother Teresa was pleased.

But he didn't want to just bring medicine. He also wanted to use his medical training to help relieve suffering there. He wanted to be a doctor to them. He wanted to *Make a Difference*. In his first meeting with her he asked Mother Teresa where he could best serve. She sent him to see Sister Priscilla, in the facility that is actually called the House for the Dying Destitutes. Gary, in his starched, buttoned-down shirt and nice slacks, shoes and stethoscope, arrived thinking this was the place where he could do the most good.

Sister Priscilla, in her soft British accent, greeted him at the door and said, "Follow me." They walked through the men's ward, which Gary described as being full of "skeletons with skin," and he wondered why they weren't stopping there. *Could there be a needier group than this?* he wondered. Then they walked through the women's ward, and the women were in a similar state – writhing in pain, moaning, too weak to eat, just moments, in some cases, from leaving this world. But they passed through that ward, too. *Why aren't we stopping? What could be worse than this?* Gary thought. Then they got to the kitchen.

I get it, Gary thought to himself. *They're going to serve me lunch first.* But they walked through the kitchen and out the back door, into a narrow, fetid alley. Sister Priscilla pointed to a very large pile of garbage. The smell triggered Gary's gag reflex.

"We need you to take this garbage down the street to the dump," she said, handing him two buckets and a shovel. "The dump is several blocks down the street on the right. You can't miss it." With a nod and a slight smile she was gone.

Gary stood there, stunned, wondering if this was a joke. Then, after a few confused moments, he tucked his stethoscope around his neck, grabbed a shovel and dug into the pile. He filled the buckets and carried them to the dump, trying to ignore the curious bystanders watching this well-dressed American doing the job of the lowest caste. He dumped out the nausea-inducing contents and returned to the pile. He did this for most of the day. He struggled with his thoughts about his talent being wasted out there in the garbage pile. He knew that his gifts and training could be better used indoors where the real suffering was occurring. He wondered why he was working on a project that was so disgusting.

By mid-afternoon, soaked in sweat, smelling like the garbage pile, he finished his task. Still confused and feeling undervalued and even insulted, he walked back to the front of the building to say goodbye to Sister Priscilla. While waiting, he saw a handwritten sign on the wall quoting Mother Teresa that said, "We can do no great things, only small things with great love." In that moment it became clear to him that no matter how much one knows, how much one has achieved, how much education one has, the real responsibility each person has is to do whatever is needed – and to do it with love.

You don't have to be a doctor to serve others.

KATRINA AND THE GIRL

When George Sisler's group of volunteers went to New Orleans in the aftermath of Hurricane Katrina, many of the volunteers were builders and carpenters who were able to tear out mold-filled walls, knock down partially destroyed structures, replace roofs, and rewire damaged electrical systems. Sisler runs a volunteer service organization called One Heart - Many Hands. This is a sister organization of Heart to Heart's, founded by Gary and his first staff member, Barbi Moore. The Katrina group was mostly full of professionals. But of all the volunteers George worked with for the two years after the storm, the one he remembers best was the thirteen-year-old daughter of one of the construction workers. When Sisler first saw her, he wasn't crazy about the idea of having her there. The sites were dangerous, full of vermin and disease, and he didn't want to have to be responsible for her safety in the rough work.

At first she stood around and watched the crew work, and did what she could to help. When she saw that the crew was creating debris piles out of the damaged homes so that bulldozers could transfer the piles to trucks to take to the landfill, a light in her head came on. Carefully, gently, she began picking through the piles before the bulldozers came. She removed pictures, trinkets, anything that looked like it could have a memory attached to it, and put it in a separate pile for the homeowner. It couldn't all be trash, she knew. Some of these things were smothered in love, and she knew the owners would be sad without them.

She was not a licensed contractor. She wasn't a trained professional. But some actions don't need special training or licenses.

From its very beginning, Heart to Heart has operated from these assumptions:

- Everyone has something to give.
- Most people are willing to give of themselves when they see the need and have the opportunity.
- Everyone can do something for someone right now.

Even though much of Heart to Heart's work has been in the medical relief field, it has always encouraged volunteers to be involved in their relief efforts regardless of training or expertise. In the Heart to Heart warehouse in Kansas, volunteers assemble disaster relief kits that go on the medical airlifts all around the world. Everyone can do something.

Dylan Aebersold is a student at MidAmerica Nazarene University in Olathe, Kansas. As a freshman he remembers walking out of church one day and being approached by a couple of students who lived in his dormitory.

"Hey," they said. "Wanna go to Haiti?"

"I thought, why not?" Dylan recalls.

During a break between semesters, a group of MNU students was going to the Cascade Pichon area of Haiti to help Heart to Heart build a clinic to treat cholera. The disease was sweeping through the mountain villages after the earthquake, and communities in that region identified health care as their chief concern. Working with these community leaders and MNU, Steve put together a plan for getting the clinic built. Volunteers from around the U.S., including the MNU students, went to the area.

Serving others is not a specialty that needs training, education, money or authority. It's a way of seeing the world differently. It's a way of living where the motivation is not necessarily to change the world. It's an awareness that a meaningful life occurs when we pay attention to what we can do, wherever we are. It's doing small things with great love.

"When I got there, I thought 'What the heck am I doing here?'" Dylan said. "My mom would be freaking out right now!"

Dylan didn't have construction or medical experience. He was told about the need, thought maybe he could offer something, and he went. Mostly, he helped prepare the spot where the clinic could be built. He carried supplies up the treacherous road that kept trucks from making it to the top of the hill. And he played with the kids. Lots of kids. And he thought to himself, "These kids need a school!"

When he returned to MNU, he said that he couldn't get Haiti out of his mind. He told his friends about how terrific the experience was, and they made a plan to go back. They saved their money and returned as Heart to Heart volunteers. While they were there, Dylan's friends saw the same need Dylan saw.

"If anyone could get a school built for this community, it would be Heart to Heart," Dylan said. "They're invested in the people there. The people in the region took us in because we were Heart to Heart volunteers."

The problem, of course, was money. While billions of dollars from around the world were being committed to earthquake and cholera relief, and much of that money was being kept by the NGOs to fund their own operations in Haiti, what were the chances of getting a school built in a part of the country that had been largely forgotten or ignored for generations?

Dylan also knew that it was not a simple proposition to go to his small, private, Christian college and ask them for help.

"We had enough trouble just raising $6,000 to help with supplies for the clinic the first trip," he said.

Steve's estimate for what was needed to build the school? $120,000. Steve challenged Dylan and the MNU students to raise the first $70,000.

"Holy crap," Dylan said.

But, sounding like a true visionary who has seen the impossible become possible, he soon changed his thinking.

"When you think about it, $70,000 is not that much money," he said. "Especially if you get students behind it."

He went to Randy Beckum, the administrator who oversees spiritual formation at the university, with a plan. If every student at the university gave $2 a week just during the school year, they'd make their goal. Which they did. Other Nazarene universities from around the country began participating. The Haitian government provided teachers, and for the first time in the region's history, the Cascade Pichon children are being educated. More about this school is described later in this book.

Dylan said he is often asked if the money he spent to volunteer in Haiti would have been better spent if it had been given directly to an agency. Why spend it on his travel expenses when he could have given all of it to the people in need?

"When you go there you see stuff you've never seen before," he said. "And when you see it for yourself, you get ideas."

Many other groups have traveled to the Cascade Pichon area and come up with even more ideas.

The Church of the Resurrection, a large Methodist church in the Kansas City area, saw the need and sent volunteers to train Haitian teachers in the region. Google provided state-of-the-art tablets, and Inveneo provided the technological infrastructure for internet connection in cooperation with Digicell, the major Haiti cell phone provider.

DEGAJE

In the Creole language of Haiti, there is a term that describes what the university students and the church volunteers have done. The word is "degaje," (pronounced *DAY-gah-JAY*) and technically it refers to any type of informal economic activity or enterprise. "Yon ti degaje," for example, is to hold a small job with a small salary. But the meaning is broader than that. The idea is that the Haitian person takes a very small opportunity that life offers him or her, and creates a bigger opportunity.

Perhaps the best definition is "To take what little you have in your hand and make something greater." Sometimes it can even mean "Make the best you can with what you have."

Haitians, from the beginning of their independence from France in the early 1800s, have had to *degaje*. Once they achieved independence, they were isolated by other world powers and their products were banned. To remove themselves from this isolation, the winner of the war – Haiti – had to pay the loser – France – billions of dollars in compensation for the lost income from the slave sugar plantations. It paid on this debt for almost 150 years. Not exactly the Marshall Plan the U.S. developed with Europe after World War II.

Very few countries have had their "freedom" controlled by outsiders, the way Haiti has experienced from other countries whose interests were definitely not pro-Haiti. Many Haitian people were forced to move off their small family farms to work in foreign-owned factories in the cities, only to have those factories close when it became more profitable for the companies to move their operations to countries such as Bangladesh, Mexico, Dominican Republic, and elsewhere.

So the word *degaje* is more than a word – it is a way of life in Haiti. It requires tenacity, courage, and a commitment to do a great deal with very little. The MNU students in particular engaged in *degaje* without even knowing the word, but they saw it in the Haitians they worked with.

But you don't have to cross an ocean to serve, or to *degaje*. In case anyone thinks that "Doing the Right Thing" means one has to leave the country, sometimes all it takes is looking in our own neighborhoods. When Andre Butler was a teenager growing up in Kansas City, he remembers being told by his grandmother to "go cut that woman's lawn." It was the yard belonging to an elderly woman in the neighborhood. Andre, the former Heart to Heart CEO, didn't want to. There was no incentive. He knew he wasn't going to get paid for it. It gets hot and humid in Kansas City in the summer. What's in it for him? But, as he said later, you listen to your grandmother, and you cut the lawn. All he got out of the deal was a cold glass of lemonade or iced tea. Looking back, he says that cutting the woman's lawn was a shaping experience for him because he learned the value of volunteering. He knew he wouldn't get any money or recognition. But he also knew that the woman could not cut the lawn herself. You can serve another even if all you have is a lawn mower.

Years later he learned that the elderly lady told her friends in the neighborhood that the visits from Andre were the highlights of her week. Cutting the grass, spending a few moments in conversation, looking her in the eye, sharing some refreshment. Small things.

In her book *Plan B*, Anne Lamott advises that serving others is something we're supposed to do as human beings. But how do you do it? Where do you start?

"First, find a path, and a little light to see by," she writes. "Then push up your sleeves and start helping."

"Every single spiritual tradition says that you must take care of the poor, or you are so doomed that not even Jesus or the Buddha can help you. You don't have to go overseas. There are people in this country who are poor in spirit, worried, depressed, dancing as fast as they can; their kids are sick, or their retirement savings are gone. There is great loneliness among us, life-threatening loneliness.... You do what you can, what good people have always done: you bring thirsty people water, you share your food, you try to help the homeless find shelter, you stand up for the underdog."[2]

Serving others is part of what it means to be a human being. Much is made in the professional world about finding one's true vocation. But vocation, as Gary and Steve see it, is much deeper than the job one might have. Vocation is more of a sense of what one is "called" to do. And in their view, the "call" on all of us is to find ways we can use our gifts, talents, time, interests, money, or whatever else, to serve others.

In his book *Wishful Thinking*, Frederick Buechner says that the problem with finding out what our "true" vocation is comes from trying to sort out what is the voice of self-interest, ego, or God. Sometimes those voices are the same, but not always.

"The kind of work God calls you to is the kind of work (a) that you need most to do and (b) that the world most needs to have done. If you really get a kick out of your work, you've presumably met requirement (a), but if your work is writing cigarette ads, the chances are that you've missed requirement (b). On the other hand, if your work is being a doctor in a leper colony, you have probably met requirement (b), but if most of your time you are bored and depressed by it, the chances are you have bypassed (a), but probably aren't helping your patients much either. The place God calls you to is the place where your deep gladness and the world's deep hunger meet."[3]

One of the core values of Heart to Heart is that serving others is something that comes from within each of us, and it is something that the world desperately needs.

The beauty of this is that we can usually find our vocation right where we are – next to us. Sometimes it's the next country, or the next apartment or the next chair over. It's not just about solving world problems. Certainly climate change, war, bullying, pollution, shortages, inequity *would* be improved if we all served each other in some small way. But it isn't always easy.

It might involve taking out the trash.

Or getting your fellow students to raise some money.

Or finding family keepsakes.

Or mowing a lawn on a hot day.

Small things.

With great love.

It's all a kind of *degaje*.

YOU'LL NEVER BE THE SAME

Chapter 4

FAITH FRIENDLY

U sually mornings are quiet in the mountain communities in Tibet. Maybe it's possible to hear prayer flags snapping in the breeze. Maybe there are workers sweeping pathways, swishing their tree-branch brooms. But this particular morning in the village of Drigung sounded different to Gary. He and two friends had been traveling through the region for a couple of weeks, asking monks for places to sleep in Tibetan Buddhist monasteries. Just before the trip Gary had knee surgery because of an injury from his deployment to Iraq, so he was on crutches, which seemed to strike the Tibetans with some curiosity. Gary freely gave them lessons in how to walk with these additional aluminum legs.

But there was commotion outside the window of the monastery's guest room this day. Hearing chanting and loud discussion, Gary woke up, hobbled to the window, and said to his friends, "You gotta see this!" Then he grabbed his crutches and headed out the door.

In the courtyard of the monastery, the body of an elderly man was on the ground. He was clearly dead. Surrounding him were monks in their traditional yellow and maroon robes, along with people from the nearby community. After prayers and more discussion, the monks wrapped the body in a blanket, and hoisted it onto a monk's shoulder. The procession headed briskly up a mountain path, with Gary and his friends close behind.

After about thirty minutes of climbing, Gary noticed the sky. It was filled with hundreds of vultures, seemingly suspended in the air above the mountain peak, like so many tiny kites. When he got to where the procession of monks ended, he saw the body stretched out on a slab of rock. After a few more minutes of prayer and chanting, a ceremony began. A man emerged from a nearby temple shrine with a machete in his hand. Quickly, methodically, the man sliced the body into pieces, tossing them onto nearby rocks.

The vultures began to descend, as if all planes circling O'Hare Airport had been given clearance to land at the same time. Some came so close to the bystanders that their wings brushed against people's shoulders as they crowded near the remains. Tibetans with sticks kept the birds a few feet away.

When the man with the machete finished, he walked away and the vultures went after the remnants of the dead man like starving people at a buffet. Within minutes, all that was left of the body was a skeleton. The man with the machete returned, but this time with an enormous stone mallet. He mashed the bones into tiny pieces, and the vultures returned for their second course.

Within about two hours there was not a trace of the body. It had all been carried skyward – which is how the procedure got its name: sky burial.

"Now that," Gary said, turning on his crutches to face his friends, "is how I want my funeral!"

Heart to Heart had done considerable work in Tibet. When they were invited to that region, the topic they were asked most about was death and dying. The Buddhist view of death, as can be seen in the sky burial, is considerably different from the view more common in the United States. But, there is always the chance to learn from one another. One of the key people who paved the way for Heart to Heart to come to Tibet was Tashi Tsering, an elderly man living in Lhasa, who has become a leader in the area. As a child Tsering was in a dance troupe that entertained the Dalai Lama in the 1950s. He was educated in the U.S., and for that he was sent to a brutal re-education camp in China for six years when he tried to return. He now runs several schools in Tibet and helps NGOs like Heart to Heart.

While the founders of Heart to Heart were firmly rooted in the Christian faith, the organization from the beginning has intentionally sought to be friendly to all faiths. Both Gary and Steve grew up with an understanding of the power of faith, and their world view is shaped by their Christian background, but that shaping has expanded, not limited, their sense of who to serve.

"We serve all people," Steve said. "There is no litmus test for love."

As important as it is to serve people of all faiths, Heart to Heart also seeks to engage volunteers from every faith tradition. There are also increasing numbers of volunteers who don't identify with any faith, but consider themselves spiritual. Many become volunteers strictly because of their humanitarian values not connected to any faith.

"We don't ignore faith," Gary said. "We respect it. We embrace it. We celebrate it!"

One of the major areas of conflict and need in the world is the Palestinian territories, which include Gaza and the West Bank. In Gaza City, Gary worked with the Red Crescent Society, the Muslim version of the Red Cross, to provide medical supplies to refugees and destitute Palestinian hospitals.

"My main contact in Palestine was Yassar Arafat's brother," Gary said. "He knew that I had just met with the Israeli version of the Red Cross, and he asked me why I was helping both sides. I told him that my Christian faith motivated me to serve the needs of the poor, whoever they are, or whatever they believe."

Mr. Arafat thought about that for a moment, took off his iconic checkered head scarf, known as a keffiyeh, embraced Gary and said, "I believe you. You are welcome here as my brother."

That encounter is a classic example of what it means to be faith friendly.

SERIOUSLY. ALL FAITHS

One of the images many people have in their minds when they think about Haiti is of voodoo – the ancient religion passed down through generations since African slaves were brought to the island. That image involves drums, animal sacrifice, gods or demons possessing people in a ceremony, and plenty of rum. The presence of voodoo in Haitian culture is so strong that observers jokingly say that 80 percent of the Haitian people are Roman Catholic, 20 percent are Protestant, but 100 percent of them practice some form of voodoo.

Voodoo temples are as common in Haiti as neighborhood churches. And when a voodoo ceremony is under way, it can be unnerving to the uninitiated. Amy Wilentz, who has written extensively about Haiti, wrote that, even though the people of Haiti are no longer slaves from the 1700s, "they worship the gods of old Africa who come down poles or up out of the earth to possess worshippers, who then spit and swing machetes at the congregation."[4] "It's as if, instead of hearing about Jesus being the embodiment of God as man, you yourself have the privilege of embodying that contradiction yourself, when the god arrives to possess you."[5]

She describes going to a voodoo ceremony, where the priest and his assistant are bent over a white enamel bowl full of cornmeal, with a candle in the middle. They sing in a language that is a combination of African dialects and Creole, a language that she says is one of the few sacred languages in existence, and that is used exclusively in voodoo ceremonies. A pole in the middle of the room has a cement snake carved around it. The singing picks up steam as the others in the room join in. There is clapping and drumming. Someone pours rum down the back of the cement snake and someone else lights the rum with a lighter, making a blue flame climb the pole. Then the fire goes out and the singing stops. "We hear next a strange, loud, guttural human noise," Wilentz writes. "Without warning, without fanfare, here is Africa handed down from the days of the colony as, before our very eyes (in a sense), Ogoun (a warrior god) comes down the pole from elsewhere to possess the priest."[6]

This kind of experience would frighten most people who aren't from Haiti. They wouldn't understand the rituals, the history, the narrative handed down from ancestors, the symbolism, the connection it makes to life in Africa before slave traders stole people by the thousands and shipped them off to Europe and the U.S. like domestic animals. They wouldn't understand that voodoo is a significant part of Haiti's political, socio-economic and cultural experience. They wouldn't understand that most of the voodoo images people in North America and Europe have are trivial representations from Hollywood, churches and politicians.

But if Heart to Heart was going to work alongside Haitian people and help to build back their country, they knew they had accept the fact that voodoo was part of the Haitian story. They couldn't pretend that it didn't exist. It had been part of Haiti's existence for centuries.

"Voodoo was something that could be understood as – most important – *not us,*" Wilentz writes. "It was other, and both seductive and alien. It was everything the white Westerner was not: exotic, African, pagan, exciting, dangerous, deep."[7]

When Heart to Heart tried to organize leadership groups in communities to provide long-term improvements in health care, they knew that faith was part of the fabric of every community, so they intentionally sought out religious leaders, including voodoo priests.

One of the first opportunities they had was in the community Place L'Or. The Catholic Church had a strong presence there, and so did the Baptist Church. And of course, voodoo was part of the community's fabric. When Heart to Heart gathered the community leaders to develop plans for providing health care, the religious leaders met in a clinic built by volunteers from the Church of the Nazarene. The subject of religion never came up.

"We share a common life together as members of the same community," said one of the voodoo leaders. "Faith is in the background of all that we do, but it is not part of the discussion about community development."

Voodoo beliefs and Christian beliefs seem incompatible – even enemies. They seem to draw on the supernatural from opposite places. They appear to have little common ground. And yet the needs of the community make the leaders set aside their differences, they said.

"When there is a disaster or an epidemic, we have to get together because everyone is involved," said the Baptist minister.

These religious leaders make a point that Gary and Steve have known all along: serving others isn't unique to one faith or another. People of all faiths, and people with no faith at all, can find meaning and purpose in their lives when they serve. At some levels of society, our different faiths are what divide us. But when something happens that affects us all, those differences aren't as significant, at least temporarily. Earthquakes don't affect one religious group while avoiding others.

At the end of one meeting that involved leaders from several faith groups, Gary took the faith-friendly notion one step further.

"I've never seen a voodoo temple," he said, looking at the local voodoo priest. "I'd like to see yours."

The priest didn't hesitate. They piled into a van and drove into a nearby community and pulled in front of a house that looked like many of the other houses in the area. Except this one had an expansive courtyard in front of the building.

The courtyard was surrounded by a concrete wall, painted blue and white. There were two fire pits with icons near each. There were also cards, books, candles, and a Bible. Some of the icons were crosses. A small chapel-like structure had chairs for about fifty people. The area looked like it could be used for a neighborhood rummage sale as easily as a religious ceremony. Within a few minutes another voodoo priest came out of the house. He wore a stylish cap, short-sleeved white designer shirt, pleated pants that were between short and long, and slip-on leather shoes with no socks. Around his neck was a gold chain. His two front teeth were framed in gold. He could have been a DJ from Miami, a major recording artist, or a pastor from a mega church, but he was the local community voodoo priest, and he was happy to see everyone.

"How does a person become a voodoo priest?" Gary asked him. "Is it a calling, a vocational decision, a family business, or what?" The priest energetically explained his education in anthropology, history and philosophy, and that his role had been passed down to him by his father.

"Voodoo is a way that keeps our ties to our native Africa," the priest said. "It's a very important connection to our past."

Steve had seen voodoo ceremonies in the past, complete with chanting in the African/Creole language, and people, apparently possessed, slithering along the ground like snakes. He had also seen the influence the priests have on their communities. Plenty of times he had seen traditional "power encounters" between voodoo and Christian leaders, where each tried to prove whose God was stronger.

"Those experiences always divided the community into two, very separate competitive forces," he said.

It was clear to Steve that if Heart to Heart was going to make any progress in engaging Haitians in their own development as a nation, voodoo had to be factored in. To not include voodoo when engaging Haitians would be like trying to develop the United States without mentioning George Washington.

Religious differences don't always have to be divisive.

WHAT REALLY MATTERS

Several years ago Gary was in Kosovo, giving medical care in communities after the NATO bombings in the area had stopped. He was called to the home of a family where the mother was ill. Gary spoke to the woman through an interpreter, and listened to her labored breathing. She talked to him about dying, and with short puffs of breath told him that she was worried about her children who would be left behind. There was great political turmoil in her country, and continued racial and religious violence in her community. Her children were at risk. In that moment Gary knew that the fact that she was Muslim and he was Christian was irrelevant. She was a mom, afraid for the condition of her children, and she knew she was going to be leaving this world.

Gary gave her medicine to ease her breathing. He knew she was dying and told her. He asked her if there was anything anyone could do for her. She said she wanted to go into the courtyard of her house. She was too weak to walk, so Gary and others picked up her chair and carried her outside. She looked heavenward and said, "I see my brother – I see my father." Gary knelt beside her and took her hand. "I will see you on the other side," he said. She died later that night.

"This was not the time to talk about our differences in faith," he said. "It was the time to talk about what we had in common – the uncertainty of the future, the love for our children."

Islam and Christianity have significant differences. They take different positions on fundamental issues such as Jesus, Scripture, Mohammed, the role of women, everyday life, and they have had those differences for hundreds of years. Wars, inquisitions, geographic divisions and countless acts of barbarism have been experienced as a result of the differences between the two religions. And yet there are other times when those differences seem less important, such as when our common humanity is at stake.

Gary learned something that night in Kosovo. Serving each other can be "faith friendly." It can, and does, include the "other," whether we understand the "other" or not. Christian. Muslim. Voodoo. No faith at all. The needs of each other transcend everything else.

When Mother Teresa encountered a dying homeless man on the streets of Kolkata who had no place to die with dignity, she didn't check to see what his religious beliefs were. She responded to the need in front of her. As she developed her ministry of caring for the dying destitute, she didn't consider whether the people in need were Catholic, Hindu, Muslim, atheist or agnostic. Need is need.

When Jesus tells the story of the Good Samaritan, it is not only a story about serving others, but it is also a story about overcoming racial and religious differences to help one another.

Heart to Heart did considerable work with Mother Teresa in India, and a personal relationship developed between Gary and the Nobel Peace-Prize winning nun. They collaborated where the Hindu religion was dominant, even to the degree of throwing a party for an entire village that had been declared "unclean" by the dominant religion. The people in the village suffered from leprosy. They had been banished to an area where they would be out of sight and mind of the local community. Mother Teresa gave Heart to Heart permission to plan a special concert for the inhabitants of the leprosy village. They brought in musicians, dancers, food and medical assistance, and threw the biggest party of the villagers' lives. The event broke down long-held social and religious barriers.

Many faiths identify certain people who they see as "unclean." Being faith-friendly means there is no barrier to anyone, regardless of faith, gender, political affiliation, social status or anything else.

"Faith friendly means that nothing should keep us from serving one another," Steve said.

A few days after Mother Teresa died in 1997, Gary called the Sisters at the Mother House in Kolkata to inquire about the funeral. "Don't bother coming," said Sister Nirmala, Mother Teresa's assistant and successor. "Don't spend the money." Gary wasn't satisfied with that response, though. He really wanted to participate in celebrating his friend's life. He told the Sister that he still wanted to come.

"Doctor, what would Mother say?" said Sister Nirmala.

"Mother would say 'don't come,'" Gary said.

Six years later Gary received an invitation to attend Mother Teresa's beatification in Rome. There were several days of events, and the Sisters gave Gary a card with a piece of Mother Teresa's sari attached to it. "It will help you pray," they said.

At the Beatification service Gary was seated in the second row at St. Peter's Cathedral, behind Mother Teresa's sister and the actress Olivia Hussey, who played Mother Teresa in the 2006 movie about her. The mass was celebrated by Pope John Paul II. When it came time for the Eucharist, Gary had a flashback to Kolkata.

He was there with several volunteers who had participated in an airlift of medical supplies to Mother Teresa's facilities. At the end of their stay they went to mass together and when it was time for the Eucharist he asked her what he should do.

"Although I'm a Christian, I'm a Protestant, and I know that the Eucharist in a Catholic mass is for Catholics only," he said. "I don't want to insult anyone. I respect the Catholic faith. What I should do?"

Mother Teresa didn't hesitate.

"Join me," she said.

So they did.

After he got home he asked a Catholic priest about it.

"In extreme cases, a priest has the authority to give permission," the priest told him. "If Mother Teresa said it was okay, and the priest said it was okay, then it was okay."

At St. Peter's, years later, he had the same dilemma. But this time there was a much bigger stage.

Gary looked toward Pope John Paul and asked himself, "What should I do?"

What would Mother say? he wondered.

She would say, "Join me," he thought.

So he received the elements, in an extremely faith-friendly moment.

"She was a lifelong Catholic and I'm a lifelong Protestant, but I didn't feel that it mattered in that moment, or in the moments when we were working side by side to save lives," he said. "Our faith motivates us to serve one another. All human beings can participate in relieving the suffering of someone else, no matter their faith."

OTHERS

While Heart to Heart isn't known as a religious organization, interfaith groups have recognized its impact across traditional faith boundaries. Gary received the Bodhisattva Award in Kansas City from the Buddhist Center and Tibetan Institute of Studies in 2009. The award says it is given to "A person who is able to reach Nirvana, but delays doing so out of compassion in order to save suffering beings. An enlightened Being motivated by great passion."

In 2006 he received the top humanitarian award from a Kansas City Muslim group called the Crescent Peace Society. In 2003 he was given the Distinguished Neighbor in Service award from the Kansas City Church of Jesus Christ of Latter-Day Saints. He was given the "Others" award by the Salvation Army. That award was named for William Booth, the founder of the Salvation Army, who would send encouragement to missionaries around the world via telegram. When the cost of sending telegrams became prohibitive, Booth altered the message to include just one word: "Others."

"The Salvation Army got it right," Gary said. "It's about others. It's not about buildings or stained glass. It's not about big or small churches. It's about others."

During his time in Kuwait at the military hospital as the U.S. troops were leaving Iraq, he explored all of the faith traditions he could find on the military base. There were plenty to choose from because the military provides a wide variety of religious traditions, and insists that they be open to any soldier. In a sense, this makes the military faith-friendly.

Gary saw this as an opportunity to learn about different faiths. He attended Adventist, LDS, Catholic and Protestant services. On Tuesday nights he attended Catholic religious instruction. On Wednesday nights he attended the Protestant Bible study. Another night he attended the Wiccan group's "Open Circle." At a Wiccan wedding, called a Hand Fast ceremony, the participants had forgotten to arrange for photos. So for a day, Gary was a Wiccan wedding photographer.

As a Nazarene missionary in Haiti in the 1970s and 80s, Steve also developed relationships with several different religious groups. His desire to serve others aligned him with the Episcopal, Roman Catholic, Pentecostal, Seventh Day Adventist and indigenous Haitian churches, along with the World Council of Churches and the Baha'i faith.

"People say they have tried to work in Haiti, but left without success," Steve said. "Early on I learned that working with various churches makes things much more successful."

Heart to Heart employs this strategy wherever they go. Usually, churches are involved in a community's disaster response. If you are working in that community, why avoid or ignore them? Heart to Heart seeks them out.

When Steve came back to Haiti with Heart to Heart after the earthquake, he rekindled his faith-friendly relationships throughout the country and added one more. He formed an alliance with the American Jewish Joint Distribution Committee (JDC) to assist victims of not only the earthquake, but also the ongoing natural disasters and humanitarian emergencies that continue to plague Haiti.

"Working with the JDC became a new and growing passion that proved we are much better when we work together," he said.

In Haiti, especially right after the earthquake, the need was more important than the differences. In Belaire, a region of Port-au-Prince that sustained considerable damage, the Church of the Nazarene has a sizable church building. When it was built in 1975, with Steve's help, the church leaders had the opportunity to use steel trusses and tin sheeting for its roof instead of concrete, which was the common practice at the time. While buildings around the church collapsed in the earthquake, this church was one of the few still standing.

When it first opened, the church thrived in its middle-class surroundings of successful businesses and attractive streets. The congregation was full of young professionals and home owners. Over the years the area became home to gangs and extreme poverty, but the church tried to maintain its service to the community. The pastor, Walliere Pierre, offered to share the building with Heart to Heart for a long-term medical center after the earthquake. For the clinic to accommodate the needs of the area, some major renovation was necessary. Heart to Heart worked with the JDC, BD, MEDCO/Express Scripts and others, to make the necessary improvements.

Now a truly faith-friendly sight is visible on the church. Along with a sign welcoming people to the Eglise du Nazareen, with its symbol of the Holy Spirit hovering over a Bible, there are two companion signs. One is from Heart to Heart International, and the other is from the American Jewish Joint Distribution Committee with a menorah symbol.

All of the world's faiths include an element of serving others. The Jewish people are told throughout the Old Testament to take care of those who can't take care of themselves. Muslims have an obligation to give to those in need. So do Hindus. Buddhists are taught that part of their duty in life is to relieve suffering. Christians are told specifically by Jesus to show mercy, feed the hungry, give the thirsty something to drink, clothe the naked, give shelter to the homeless, and visit the sick and those in prison. This is a common thread in most religious belief.

The Talmud says, "Therefore, when you save one life it is as if you saved the entire world."

Still, there are so many aspects that keep religions separate from one another, making it nearly impossible for different faiths to work together. But they can be united on at least this one thing. For the sake of the world, for the sake of a common human condition, their differences can be set aside at least temporarily to focus on what is before them. Needs trump creeds every time.

And sometimes, when serving others, one can even discover a faith that has been lost.

Art Fillmore was a volunteer on the Heart to Heart airlift to Vietnam. He was a religious man before he became part of the U.S. combat forces there in 1969, and then left his faith – or perhaps his faith left him -- during the carnage and the brutality he participated in. For more than twenty-five years after the war he experienced nightmares, where a ghoulish creature would rise out of the ground and read off the names of his fellow soldiers – soldiers he had seen killed or whose limbs had been blown off. It was a horrifying experience for him to try to sleep each night.

Through mutual friends, Art met Gary and Gary invited him to be the volunteer chairman of the airlift. Art said he was too filled with hate and fear. Gary reminded him that in the Sermon on the Mount, Jesus told his followers to "Love your enemies." Skeptical, Art agreed to go.

Returning to Vietnam was an emotional and deep experience for him. But it wasn't just the act of returning to the very sites of firefights that he found the most profound. That came when the Heart to Heart volunteers visited a region in Vietnam that was home to people with leprosy. It was an area filled with the country's true untouchables.

"It was the dirtiest place imaginable," he said. What moved him most wasn't the suffering of those afflicted with leprosy, though. It was the children. He felt that he saw the face of God in the children.

"The kids were healthy," he said. "It was their parents who had leprosy. And no one EVER visited them." The volunteers brought the children paper, crayons, toys, and rice.

Later, the family of the village chief asked the volunteers to come to the chief's hut and offer a prayer. Standing around his bed, Catholics, Protestants and Jews prayed for this Buddhist chief. Art was in that circle.

When he returned to the U.S., Art noticed that two things had happened since he had gone back to Vietnam to serve his enemies.

His nightmares stopped.

His faith returned.

Chapter 5

BE PRESENT

Tony Petrehn is a contractor in Johnson County, Kansas, one of the wealthiest suburbs in the U.S. When he heard about the earthquake in Haiti, he felt helpless at first as he watched the news coverage of the devastation and the suffering.

"It was conflicting, because here I was surrounded by all this wealth," he said. "Plus, I was in the middle of doing a massive home remodeling project for a client, and I knew I needed to finish that job before I could think about helping in Haiti. I have everything I need here. I'm helping wealthy people increase the size of their houses, increasing the value of their assets, and I'm watching people very close to our country who had very little, and even that was taken away."

Tony heard that volunteers were dropping everything and working with Heart to Heart, and he was drawn to the idea. He even gingerly brought up the subject to his client.

"My customer was glad I was considering this," he said. "He encouraged me to go and said the house project could be completed any time. Then I talked to the banker, and *he* wanted me to go. It was like, for a moment, everyone's priorities re-aligned and said this was the right thing."

Tony didn't have medical skills that he could use in the immediate aftermath of the earthquake. What he found he *could* do, though, was sit with people in pain as they waited to be seen by a doctor. He sat with a woman who was brought to a medical tent by her son, who had balanced her on the handlebars of his bicycle. She had been trapped under some rubble, and when she was finally rescued, her mangled foot was in desperate need of attention. She was in extreme pain.

Tony sat with her in the triage line for hours, unable to speak her language, but communicating his concern. By the time she had her wounds cleaned and treated later in the day, she sought him out and hugged him. No words were necessary.

"I knew she was the reason I had come to Haiti," he said.

Sometimes the best service we can provide for one another is presence. Our presence. This principle of coming alongside one another is a time-honored one throughout civilization. In times of need, often the best gift we can give one another is to simply be present. It is a way of saying, even to strangers, "You aren't alone." Presence leads to encouragement, which leads to hope. And sometimes, hope is the difference between life and death.

In the Jewish tradition there is a practice called *shiva*. When a person dies, mourners come to the family's home to "sit shiva."

That means they come alongside the grieving people and mourn with them. No words need to be exchanged. It is an act of solidarity that says "I acknowledge your grief. I can't fix it, but I can sit beside you as you go through it." Sometimes this is one of the greatest gifts we can give one another.

For a humanitarian organization like Heart to Heart, sitting shiva with disaster victims isn't always the first priority. Getting immediate medical aid to victims is the first order of business. But Gary and Steve and the thousands of volunteers who have represented Heart to Heart around the world know that simply being present is about as crucial as the medical relief. For some of the volunteers, it's the only thing they can reasonably do.

In the movie *Lars and the Real Girl*, the main character (Lars, played by Ryan Gossling) is a delusional young man who has difficulty establishing relationships, even with people who care deeply about him. He eventually orders an inflatable doll from the Internet, and he begins taking the doll with him to social events, has her sit at the table with him, talks to her as if she's real, and wants his friends and family to also consider her a "real girl." As Lars experiences the love of some of the people in his community, it becomes clear to him that he might not need this fictional girl as much, and so he develops a story that "Bianca," the doll, is dying. He is still very attached to her, though, and begins to grieve the doll's passing.

His family and church community could have dismissed him as being slow-minded or even just creepy. Instead, they observe their friend in pain and decide to participate in it with him. In one scene, "Bianca" is on the bed, and Lars is trying to keep her comfortable. Then he hears his door bell ring. He opens it and three women from his church walk in, uninvited. They find chairs in his living room and sit down. They each have brought bags of knitting materials. Lars stares at them, and with his face the audience can tell he is wondering why they are there.

"Well, that's how life is, Lars," says one of the ladies.

"Everything at once," says another.

"We brought casseroles," says a third.

"Thank you," says Lars. He looks around, still a little confused. The three ladies are immersed in their sewing and needlepoint. "Is there something I should be doing right now?"

"No, dear. You eat."

"We came over to sit."

"That's what people do when tragedy strikes."

"They come over, and sit."[8]

Those ladies knew that all they could do for Lars, in his delusional but grieving state, was to simply be present for him. In that moment, it was enough.

This is something each of us can do in our neighborhoods, families and communities. When the opportunity arises to be present with someone in need in another country like Haiti or China, that's worth doing. But we don't have to travel far to find someone to sit with.

Sometimes being present has a more purposeful agenda, as it did for the women in Rosalie Bertell's essay "In What Do I Place My Trust?" Bertell was a cancer researcher and reformer. She recounted how her mother, a newlywed in Washington D.C. just after World War I, noticed that many black women who had worked all day in white people's homes had trouble catching a bus to take them to their own homes.

"If there were only blacks at the corner, the buses would not stop," Bertell said. Some of the women would stand at the corner for more than an hour.

"My mother went down every evening to stand with the black women so that the buses would stop – until the drivers got the point."[9]

NEW EYES

Ed Overholt, one of the doctors who have volunteered with Heart to Heart throughout China, has taken each of his three children on airlifts and service trips to that region.

"I wanted my family and I to see the world as human beings with lives filled with hopes and dreams and needs just like we are," he said. "I wanted all of us to see the world with new eyes. Coming to China is about more than new foods, new places or new people. It's about reopening myself to people's needs, their hearts, seeing them through Christ's eyes."

Ed recalled that a representative from the Sichuan Ministry of Health made a comment at dinner that has stayed with him. The official said he thought the most important thing that the Heart to Heart delegates gave to his province was the experience to meet Americans, to see what they were really like and to see what was in their hearts firsthand since often this will be their only chance to meet an American.

"I guess these trips are a sort of 'eye exchange' program and both parties will see better forever because of it," Ed said.

When it comes to serving others, there are times when you just have to be there to be part of the new life that is dawning. Christophe Rodrigue, the Haitian we met in chapter one who works with Heart to Heart, knows firsthand that "being there" with a community, especially, is something that needs to occur before real needs can be revealed. Christophe grew up in Fondwa, was educated in community development in France, then returned to Haiti to work with peasants, farmers and agricultural governmental institutions, focusing on land distribution and improving living conditions.

"The community is like a baby; you have to raise it," he said. "You need to be there constantly, holding its hand and helping it through."

After the 2010 earthquake, Christophe left Haiti for life in the United States. However, he felt drawn back to help his people in Fondwa. Upon his return to Haiti, Christophe set up programs to come alongside the people – focusing on ways of providing food for them.

"The lesson I learned from this is that when we are facing a problem, the best solution isn't to flee, but to find other people, put our heads together, and find ways to solve that problem."

He is now the country director of Haiti for Heart to Heart.

"The objective of Heart to Heart is not to just go there, do something and leave, but to do something *with* the community," he said. "Many times projects aren't successful because organizations just go in and do those projects. They have to *involve* the community and give them responsibility for this to be successful."

Or, as one Haitian told a Heart to Heart volunteer, "Dream *with* us, not *for* us."

A few months after the earthquake, Steve visited Cascade Pichon (mentioned in chapter three) with Christophe, his new Heart to Heart colleague, along with a local pastor, Samerite Desruisseaux. The route was an unclimbable steep incline. It was so primitive that although Pastor Samerite kept referring to it as a road, Christophe said that "this road isn't fit to be called a goat trail." In a fit of frustration, Steve declared that his truck would not continue. The terrain was tearing his Toyota 4Runner to pieces.

But they finally arrived at the base of the falls, and found that more than 350 people had gathered in anticipation of their visit. Many had been waiting several hours. After talking with the people, Steve and Christophe asked them what they needed most. They said they needed a doctor. They said that there had never been a doctor working in that area. Steve said something that he imagined Gary would say.

"We'll come back, and we'll bring doctors," he said. "But for us to return, you have to make that road passable for our vehicles."

The Haitians replied in a pragmatic way.

They said they would be glad to fix the road, but they didn't have any tools.

Christophe worked with one of his home-town organizations, The Peasants of Fondwa, to provide shovels, picks and wheel barrows.

Nearly 300 people of the Cascade Pichon area worked from June until October to improve the road. When Steve arrived that autumn with Haitian doctors, not only was the site at the base of the falls beautiful, but so was the sight of hundreds of people, some of whom had walked five hours, all gathered to greet them.

"I'll never forget that sight," Steve said.

The doctors used a person's house for a makeshift clinic, but it was clear that a permanent structure would be needed. Construction of this type needs lots of rocks, sand, cement, steel rebar and a great deal of water.

Pastor Samerite worked with local public officials to organize hundreds of Haitian volunteers into a public works group to bring the materials to the work site.

"It was unbelievable," Steve said. "As we watched the people carry these heavy rocks on their heads from greater and greater distances from the work site, one of the public officials said to me, 'I have never in all my life seen people work this hard or this fast.'"

Steve asked the official, "Why do you think they are working so hard and fast?"

The official stopped one of the workers – a woman who was carrying three rocks on her head.

"Why are you carrying three rocks at a time when it would be easier to carry one or two?" he asked her. "And why are you walking so fast?"

Steve said the woman looked at the man as only a regular person can look at a politician, and replied, "Because we really need this clinic." And then she hurried on her way.

The clinic was completed in record time. The local volunteers brought all of the water, all of the sand, all of the rocks. They dug the foundation and carried the sacks of cement from the drop-off point on the road where the supply trucks had to stop, about three miles from the work site.

Once the clinic was established and operational, the volunteers focused on something far more long term. They planted trees. Thousands and thousands of them.

LISTENING

Haiti was once a beautiful, lush paradise, filled with spectacular mahogany and other hardwood trees. At that time, Haiti was the largest exporter of sugar cane of any country in the world. Then came centuries of exploitation and abuse. Initially, the trees were cut and sent back to France and other countries. More recently, the trees were cut because Haitians cook with charcoal, and charcoal is made from wood. The only wood available is from the few trees that remain. Haiti is now largely a barren wasteland of treeless, eroded mountains.

The volunteers are not only planting trees, but they are also standing guard over them until they are big enough to withstand the goats that would devour the seedlings in a single meal. Every time the volunteer organization accumulates some money, it is spent on planting more trees. The goal is that, in the not too distant future, these trees will provide shade for the coffee plants that are being grown in the area. Trees hold down the top soil and prevent erosion. The coffee plants will one day provide income that is so desperately needed to provide an adequate standard of living for the hundreds of coffee growers in the area.

In Cascade Pichon, Christophe is helping develop the community with sustainable programs including health care, literacy programs, civil training lessons, road improvements, water purification, increased coffee production, tree planting and more, and replicating those efforts elsewhere.

"We need people like Heart to Heart to go to our communities, meet the people, find out their needs, find out their resources, and find a way to work together," he said. "But we also need to consider that each person, farmer or family has ideas on how best to do things. They have the experience. You can learn a lot just by listening."

But you can't really listen without being present. Heart to Heart's staff in Haiti understands this. They understand the importance of being present in the communities where they serve. They participate in local community events by attending funerals, weddings, graduations and significant birthday celebrations on their own time and at their own expense. Like Tony, foreigners from all over the world come to Haiti to volunteer, to serve, to be present. In the same way, Haitian volunteers cross deeply rooted social and cultural barriers to volunteer, to serve and to be present.

Two college students, Erik Unruh and Zach Phillips, experienced the power of presence when they went to Guatemala to help with community development and water purification efforts. The part of Guatemala where they were working was a strange juxtaposition of wealth and poverty. They were in the region of Lake Atitlan, a popular resort area where travelers from all over the world come to enjoy the beauty of this volcano filled with water, surrounded by other volcanoes. But, as is typical of most resort areas around the world, Lake Atitlan's neighboring communities are filled with indigenous people living in serious poverty. Many of these people struggle for life's basic necessities, like clean water, food, and adequate health care.

Erik and Zach were part of a group of MidAmerica

Nazarene University students who were volunteering with Heart to Heart. In one of the communities, called Patanatic, the people there told the boys of a plan they had been working on to build a health care clinic in their area.

"They had already talked with people about the amount of concrete, lumber and other supplies they would need," Zach said. "They had the laborers to build it, and a lot of the suppliers said they'd donate materials. They just needed some help covering what wasn't being donated."

Community leaders estimated that the materials would cost around $50,000.

"On the one hand, $50,000 seems like a lot of money," Zach said. "But when you compare it to a professional athlete's salary, or the cost of the cars driven by the parents of some of our students, it doesn't seem that much. It wouldn't buy a small piece of medical equipment in the U.S., but it could build a clinic for an entire region? We had to try."

Zach and Erik talked with Randy Beckum, one of Mid-America's leaders, mentioned in chapter three, about whether it would be possible for the students to raise that much money.

"I knew these students," Randy said. "They weren't saying 'God told us to do this.' They were saying, 'There's a need – can we help these people?' My philosophy is that if students have a dream, then the answer is yes until there is a reason to say no."

Randy and the students brainstormed as to how to do it.

They calculated that if their entire student body of about 1,000 gave $2 each week, they'd have $30,000 by the end of the semester. But they knew that every student wouldn't, or couldn't, commit to that. They approached the university's board of trustees and asked if they would match whatever the students raised. The board agreed.

Zach and Erik made a presentation to the student body in a chapel service, and then gave weekly updates. Tuesday chapel services became known as $2 Tuesdays. Even on weekends when high school students came to campus as part of the admissions department's recruiting efforts, the high schoolers were told about the clinic and asked to participate – which they did.

By the end of the school year the students, trustees, staff, faculty and those considering becoming students raised $65,000. The local Rotary chapter got involved, and so did local medical technology companies, and so did the group Engineers Without Borders.

The clinic was built and is now staffed by Guatemalan doctors, nurses, and volunteers. One floor of the clinic is a community center, another is the medical floor, another is a volunteer center, and on the roof is a community garden. After graduating with a nursing degree from MidAmerica, Erik moved to Patanatic for a few months and worked in the clinic as a volunteer.

"One of the things I learned from this is that people often

go into a community to serve, but they have pre-conceived ideas on what the community needs," Zach said. "When we do that, then service is still all about me, and how I feel about it. But this community had already established that they needed a clinic, and we were able to plug into that. If we were focused on what we were going to do for them, well, we would have missed what they really needed."

GRILLING AND DANCING

The Guatemala experience for Zach and Erik was a logical extension of what they had been already doing as college students in previous years. Even as freshmen at MidAmerica, they got the idea to spend Sunday evenings in downtown Kansas City among homeless people, with no agenda beyond wanting to eat with them. They brought a grill.

"We knew we were going to eat on Sunday nights, so why not eat in the park downtown and see who else wanted to eat with us?" Erik said. "We wanted to do something that we don't do in our everyday life."

For weeks the students went downtown, grilled some hamburgers and hot dogs, and shared what they had with the people who lived in the park. Pretty soon they were handing out eighty-five meals each week, holding benefit concerts to pay for the supplies, and giving away clothing.

"It was the kind of thing where people wanted to participate," Erik said. "All we were doing was eating together."

Erik and Zach saw the impact of their actions on a park for a few hours a week. Then they saw the impact of their actions in a community in Guatemala. What they didn't count on was the impact on their own college campus.

"MidAmerica was struggling financially while we were trying to raise money for this clinic," Randy said. "Zach and Erik helped redirect us to our real purpose in the world, which is to make a difference by being regularly generous. We calculated what the clinic cost each student per week, and it came to about $1.46. When you think about it, it's not that much."

But the idea caught on. Now, each year, the students decide what else they are going to get involved in. One year it was a food program for new mothers in Zambia. Another year it was an orphanage in Kenya. It was one of the influences that inspired Dylan Aebersold, mentioned in chapter three.

"Now when we think about doing something, we're used to it – we know we've done this before, and it's part of our practice," Randy said.

But it all starts by going somewhere – showing up and, to put it delicately, shutting up. Being present doesn't mean we do all the talking, or even all the "doing."

Paul Farmer, one of the most successful people to deliver aid to Haiti through his organization Partners in Health, knows that this is the best kind of assistance.

"The most efficient and effective way to engage in this

work is to accompany the intended beneficiaries," he wrote. "To accompany someone is to go somewhere with him or her, to break bread together, to be present on a journey with a beginning and an end. It means listening, working alongside communities, walking with them until their goals become their reality."[10]

The Guatemala experience had at least one other surprising result for Zach. More than a year after the clinic was built, he was in a little restaurant in Kansas City where the music was loud and the dancing vigorous. He was wearing the Heart to Heart shirt he had been given while volunteering in Patanatic.

"A guy came up to me and asked if I worked with Heart to Heart," Zach said, laughing. "It was really noisy in there and we were shouting to hear each other. I told him that I had volunteered with Heart to Heart in Guatemala."

The guy told Zach that he was a student at Kansas University, and that he had seen a video about what the MNU students had done, and recognized Zach from the video. The guy and his friends were so inspired by the video that they went to Patanatic to volunteer, and now his group was raising money to help support the clinic.

"He told me, 'If a small school like MidAmerica can do something like this, then we should be doing something, too,'" Zach said. "KU is now helping staff the clinic."

Chapter 6

BETTER TOGETHER

I t seems like common sense to say that efforts to serve others are more effective when we collaborate instead of compete with each other. But common sense isn't always the common experience.

In the days immediately following the 2010 earthquake in Haiti, the soccer stadium in downtown Port-au-Prince became the main triage area for the sick and injured. Medical personnel from around the world set fractures, stitched wounds, gave antibiotics, removed foreign objects, and sent those who needed surgery and amputations to whatever was left of local hospitals. The needs were immediate and people were desperate.

The stadium had become a refugee camp and everyone there needed something in addition to medical care: water and food. Supplies began running low within the first few days.

Gary could see the situation deteriorating almost by the hour. He knew the need was serious, and he could see how out of control the area could become if supplies weren't replenished soon. He remembered that, when he flew in to the military base in Port-au-Prince, he saw pallet after pallet of food and water sitting on the tarmac. The supplies had been brought in by the U.S. military, and he knew that they were still developing a plan to distribute them. With the chaos on the roads and the lack of coordination among agencies, he could envision that those supplies could remain on the tarmac while people a few miles away desperately needed them.

Similar to food and medicine scarcity he had seen around the world, he knew that this wasn't really a matter of shortage. This was a matter of distribution.

Using his position as a colonel in the U.S. Army Reserve, Gary called the base and requested that the food and water be brought to the soccer stadium immediately. With order rapidly deteriorating, the military decided that it would be too dangerous to send the supplies on the roadways. Instead, the military arranged for the U.S. Navy to fly it in via helicopter. There was an Army helicopter available, but the Navy CH-53 Sea Stallion chopper could hold more supplies.

Before long, a large U.S. Army truck arrived at the stadium, and twenty-five soldiers hopped off. Their orders were to secure an area where the Navy helicopter could land. Gary introduced himself to them, and they established a landing zone in the stadium's ample parking lot. It was flat and paved – perfect for a landing spot. The plan was to get people to line up in the area outside the stadium, wait for the helicopter to land, receive a

Meal Ready to Eat (MRE) and a bottle of water, and then move on. It was a good plan. Volunteers and the soldiers organized the enormous crowd into an orderly queue.

Gary went back into the stadium to check on the patients he had been treating, and within a few minutes the noise of agony was replaced by the roar of the approaching helicopter. Gary went back out to the landing zone to watch the descent, happy that his connections to the military could at least temporarily relieve some of the discomfort the Haitians were experiencing. The line for the desperately needed food and water snaked around the stadium. Relief was at hand.

Sort of.

The Sea Stallion came in slowly, dropping lower and lower, but didn't immediately land. Instead, it moved past the stadium wall and hovered over the stadium itself, not the parking lot. Gary and the Army personnel tried waving to direct it back to the secured landing zone, but the aircraft dropped lower over the stadium, its 130 mph downward wind from the rotors blowing tents and medical supplies skyward.

"Can't you talk to them?" Gary shouted at the troops. "Can't you get them on the radio?"

"No," he was told. "They're Navy and we're Army – they're on different radio frequencies and our radios aren't compatible."

When the helicopter landed in the stadium, the orderly line outside broke into chaos as people rushed back in. There were twenty soldiers outside, and five inside with Gary. He could see the potential disaster of having the helicopter overrun by thousands of desperate people.

The soldiers rushed in, this time with the Army truck. Soldiers pointed their weapons at the crowd and secured the helicopter from a developing riot. Other soldiers removed the pallets from the helicopter and put them on the truck, and slowly transported them all back into the parking lot. Then the Sea Stallion lifted off and returned to the base.

People got back in line, received nourishment, and inside the stadium the workers retrieved and re-assembled their tents, tarps and tables.

It was agonizing to watch. All of the volunteer work that had been blasted to bits, all of the organizing of bringing in supplies to relieve suffering, had almost blown up in Gary's face. It was a powder keg of desperate need, and this very nearly lit the match. Gary had good intentions and connections. The Army and Navy had good intentions and the means to accomplish the goal. The helicopter was a Navy asset. The personnel were Army. The supplies were from the Department of Defense. And because the groups weren't working together, they made the situation worse.

Looking at the chopper in the middle of what was once a makeshift medical center, and the debris surrounding it, Gary shook his head. "If we could only learn how to coordinate these pieces," he thought. "We'd be so much better if we worked together."

This has been a problem for some time in Haiti. Actually, it's a problem around the world. Collaboration instead of competition is one of the crucial ingredients in getting the appropriate supplies to the appropriate needs. Without collaboration and coordination, hundreds of thousands of people are affected, and many of them die.

When the earthquake hit, different non-governmental organizations had different supplies and functions from others, and part of the challenge was figuring out who had what, and how much the different groups were willing to work together. Timothy Schwartz, an anthropologist, was in the city of Leogane, the quake's epicenter, a few days after the disaster. He wrote about trying to help coordinate efforts among the different groups in that very city.

"Hundreds of wounded are pouring in and Leogane has all these organizations with different capacities and supplies. The Spanish Red Cross has water makers. The Austrian Red Cross has latrines and pumps. The French at MSF (Doctors Without Borders) have meds and a laboratory for blood work. The Japanese are the only ones with an x-ray machine, but the Germans are bringing another. The Cubans have four surgery rooms, twenty general practitioners, and five orthopedic surgeons. Heart to Heart at the Nazarene Church has pharmaceuticals, vaccines, and disposable medical supplies; and on and on."[11]

With all of these supplies and people who dropped everything to come to Haiti to help, one might think that there was a practice of sharing and cooperating. There was cooperation, but it wasn't the most common practice. Many of the aid groups appeared to be competing with one another for aid money and for media attention. Some even criticized each other publicly. It would have been better if the groups had worked together.

THEORY OF COOPERATION

Ironically, while the aid organizations might not have been working together, the Haitian people were.

Within a few years, as Heart to Heart moved beyond the disaster phase of aid, the Haitian people themselves offered a unique way forward.

Leaders from business, government, religious and cultural groups began to gather and identify their communities' concerns. They called their groups "federations," and they worked together to implement a plan to address those concerns.

The federation concept is actually an old one in Haiti, but was rarely implemented. The idea was developed by the government of Haiti in the 1980s, but was mostly a theory of cooperation with little practical application. The theory continued to be fleshed out over the years and the federation concept became a part of the national strategy for developing the country. But mostly, the federations were nothing more than a means for labor unions and other groups to gather and work together.

Steve saw a bigger potential. What if a community could pull together its political leaders to identify its needs? And what if the community's religious leaders did the same? And what about the different civic groups and associations in the community? What if their leaders, together, could identify their community's needs? And then, what if the educated professionals of a community got involved? Many of them had moved to the capital city and other countries because of lack of opportunity. But what if they could be reached and asked to participate in the development of these community federations?

And then, what if representatives from each of those four groups could gather in one place to discuss how to improve their communities? And once the needs have been identified, what if they devised a plan and then took ownership to implement it?

After the earthquake Steve proposed the idea to the Haitian people he had met over the years. It was received with enthusiasm. He and representatives from each of the four groups began meeting in dozens of different communities. The political groups included mayors and other locally elected officials. Steve invited representatives from all of the local faiths, including leaders from Protestant, Catholic and Voodoo religions. "This is the first time in my thirty-five years as a Voodoo Priest that I have ever been invited to a meeting like this," one of the leaders said. Steve also met with association and professional groups. His message was always the same: If Heart to Heart was going to assist in this community, a federation needed to be formed, made up of leaders from all four sectors of the community.

Once the federation is formed and officially registered with the appropriate government agency, an executive committee is elected and gives direction to the operation of the group. By law, land can be donated or sold to the federation (not Heart to Heart), to build a clinic, school, water project or whatever that local community decides is the priority.

One of the first federations formed was in a remote area in the mountains called Cascade Pichon. The federation's first task was to identify the needs of the region. Cascade Pichon was a community that had been ignored for generations, even though it was home to a spectacular waterfall that former president Baby Doc Duvalier declared would someday be one of the country's main tourist attractions. He made that declaration in the 1970s.

Until recently, the area didn't have a school or medical clinic. Digicell, the nation's largest cell phone provider, built its area cell tower further down the mountain from Cascade Pichon because it didn't think more than a few hundred people lived further up. When the federation canvassed the area, it found more than 15,000 living above the tower.

When cholera swept through the country after the earthquake, federation representatives went to Cascade Pichon and found that cholera was not only rampant, it was going untreated. There was no medical care available that was closer than a three-hour walk down the mountain to the nearest government health center. And if one has cholera, he or she is never up for a three-hour walk. Many died trying to make that trip. The area is also virtually inaccessible by car or truck. The one road leading to Cascade Pichon, mentioned in chapter 5, is dirt and gravel, rutted, strewn with boulders, along a dry river bed, with hard right and left turns that can snap necks and shred tires.

The federation identified health care as its chief concern for the area, and they contacted Heart to Heart. Plans for a medical clinic began. Volunteers from Haiti and North America hauled supplies up the final steep, treacherous miles because the road was not passable for supply vehicles. The volunteers even carried the clinic's examination tables up the path. The tables weighed several hundred pounds each.

Samerite Deruisseaux, the federation president, had built a small hotel at the top of the mountain to accommodate the hoped-for tourists who would eventually want to see the falls.

When the clinic was completed in 2012, Heart to Heart sent Haitian doctors and nurses, and volunteer doctors from the U.S. and Mexico, to the clinic where, during the worst of the epidemic, they treated more than 100 patients per day.

They also trained additional medical personnel to work in the clinic. Federation members spread the word throughout the community as to when the clinic would be open, and on clinic days hundreds of people from the surrounding area come for treatment. The visiting Heart to Heart doctor works in Cascade Pichon for a few days, then moves to another clinic in another community for a few days. The doctor, nurse and pharmacist treat cholera, malnutrition, worms, tuberculosis, burns, and sexually transmitted diseases.

After overseeing the medical clinic's development, the federation then turned its sights on the lack of education for the thousands of children in the area. Federation census takers discovered that 95 percent of the residents were illiterate. So they set out on the seemingly impossible task of building a school in the middle of the mountains, where no school had ever existed. They also developed a plan to improve access to the area by improving the road. The land was purchased by the federation in partnership with New York University at Albany. The Haitian government provided funding for teachers. Construction of the school was funded by foundations, MidAmerica Nazarene University and individuals. It was the biggest project ever undertaken in the Cascade Pichon region. Local leadership identified the need, and then took the initiative to address that need.

Slowly but surely, the road into Cascade Pichon is improving, and so are the lives of the people.

The federation approach is an effective way to solve communities' concerns, because working together is better for the community than competing. Often communities compete for limited resources. Religious groups compete with civic groups which compete with government groups, and on and on. But the federation idea turns the premise around. Instead of each group carving out a piece of a very small pie, the leaders from the different groups meet to prioritize the needs of the community.

As Steve reminds us, "We're better together."

Working with the federations in Haiti is one of the ways Heart to Heart has been different from other aid groups in the country. Some of the strongest federations developed out of a collaboration between Heart to Heart and the Church of the Resurrection in Kansas.

"The key to the success of the federations is developing leaders," Steve said. "The partnership with Church of the Resurrection has allowed us to do additional leadership training, resulting in strong community development."

WHEN HELPING HELPS

Working with other groups has been the guiding principle for Heart to Heart since it began in 1992.

Heart to Heart started as a joint project with the Olathe, Kansas Rotary Club to remodel a YWCA facility in Belize. It ramped up quickly the second year. The agency did a humanitarian airlift to Russia, a Cold War enemy. They got medical supplies and pharmaceuticals from major corporations, and filled an Air Force cargo plane with 160 pallets that weighed more than 150,000 pounds, valued at more than $5 million. Supplies went to 34 hospitals in Russia. At the time it was one of the largest airlifts in the history of the U.S. government. On that airlift they worked with the American Academy of Family Physicians (AAFP), whose doctors quickly saw the benefit of using their expertise to assist their former adversary.

"Without the AAFP's involvement, I don't think Heart to Heart would exist today," Gary said. "They loaned us their credibility, which was like getting the Good Housekeeping Seal of Approval. When a letter to pharmaceutical companies came from them asking for donations for this airlift, that opened the doors. We still had to perform, but they got us considered. Now Heart to Heart is one of the major recipients of pharmaceutical donations in the world."

Heart to Heart has conducted massive airlifts to every conceivable region ever since.

Their airlift into Vietnam, with a FedEx cargo plane, was the first non-military U.S. plane to land in that country since the end of the war between the two countries. Vietnam officials claim that the airlift contributed significantly to normalizing relations with the U.S. The same could happen with Cuba before long. But Heart to Heart has always depended on two things to bring relief to suffering people: volunteers and partnerships.

When Heart to Heart started working in India, they worked with Mother Teresa. When they worked in China, they worked with the Sichuan Province Ministry of Health. When they worked in New Orleans after Hurricane Katrina, they worked with local emergency management officials to get supplies to the neediest areas. It has been one of the keys to Heart to Heart's success – collaboration is better than competition. It's better together. Serving others takes cooperation.

More organizations in the U.S. have seen the effectiveness of "better together," and they are working with Heart to Heart at significant levels. Jon North, the former CEO of Heart to Heart, remembers his first discussion with the American Jewish Joint Distribution Committee (JDC).

"They came to us requesting medicine for Holocaust survivors in former Soviet republics," he said. "We worked with them on that project, and then Haiti happened." The JDC began working with Heart to Heart in multiple regions within days after the earthquake.

FedEx has been a partner with Heart to Heart for more than twenty years.

"FedEx is as passionate about helping the needy as we are," North said. "They see that we can do things they can't do, and vice versa. They've been one of our greatest relationships."

After the Haiti earthquake, the president of FedEx called Heart to Heart and asked for help. Medical groups in Memphis, the corporate headquarters, were anxious to get doctors and medicine to the country, but they were having trouble getting their materials through customs, the executive said.

"It wasn't a Heart to Heart project – it wasn't us at all – but they called us for help," North said. "It's about partnership. We got it through customs for them."

Johnson & Johnson, Welch Allyn, BD, Bayada Home Health Care, FedEx, JDC, AAFP, and on and on, all collaborate with Heart to Heart to get the best possible care to the neediest people.

Competition has its place in society. It can make products better, prices lower, and service more efficient. But when it comes to serving others, competition can sometimes keep the products and services away from the people who need them most. In Haiti the objective was to save lives and improve conditions, not move merchandise. The groups there accomplished more by working together, because they're better together.

PARTNERS IN LIFE

Paul Farmer, the doctor and anthropologist mentioned in previous chapters, has spent much of his medical career in Haiti treating AIDS, tuberculosis, malaria and other epidemics. He has done the same in Rwanda, Peru and Russia, always focusing on population groups that don't have the means to fight these diseases. The term "Partners" in his organization's name, Partners in Health, is a strategic one. In a commencement speech at Northwestern University two years after the earthquake, he encouraged the audience to learn how to "harness the power of partnership."

"Partnership has been the font of our work since it began. Sometimes, these are partnerships among service providers, teachers, and researchers. Always they are partnerships among people from very different backgrounds (within one country or across many). Sometimes the partnerships link different sorts of medical expertise – surgical, medical, psychiatric, and so on. Sometimes they bring together people who design and build hospitals with those who know how to power them with renewable energy or link them to the information grid. Sometimes they link talented students around the globe... Above all, such partnerships link those who can serve with those who need services."[12]

This is easier said than done, of course. Partnerships take work, because most of us are trained in the model of scarcity, of limited supply, of competition, and in doing things ourselves. Individualism and competition are basic elements in modern society. Farmer addresses this issue later in the same speech.

"Partnerships are not always easy to maintain. Often competition rules when collaboration should prevail... Your own success will not come without real partnership. Do not think of it as coming at the cost of someone else's success. As new challenges arise to the survival of all dwellers on this planet, your generation, more than any other, will need to embrace partnership." [13]

A great example of partnership is a laboratory technician training program throughout Haiti that BD supports through funding and volunteers. In collaboration with the Haiti national lab and the U.S. Centers for Disease Control and Prevention, technicians are trained to World Health Organization standards.

Pastor Samerite in Cascade Pichon, has expanded the "togetherness" vision to help coffee growers in the region form a co-op so that they can work for better prices and higher wages. For coffee to grow well, it needs shade to grow in, so the co-op has also been responsible for planting thousands of trees in a deforested area. An individual coffee grower couldn't do that. But hundreds of coffee growers can.

Heart to Heart has promoted these partnership principles from the very beginning. In Haiti, especially, the federations have put collaboration into practice. The result is that lives are being saved, children are being educated, farmers are pooling their resources, trees are being planted, and conditions are slowly improving.

Working together can make the difference between an epidemic going untreated and saving many lives. It can make the difference between landing a helicopter inside a stadium and making matters worse, or landing it outside the stadium.

There is a Hasidic parable where a rabbi asks God about heaven and hell. God said, "I will show you hell," and he took the rabbi into a room that smelled of such a wondrous stew that it made the rabbi's mouth water. In the middle of the room was a round table, and in the middle of the table was the pot of stew. "How could this be hell?" the rabbi wondered. Then he heard the screaming. The people around the table were starving, but their spoons had very long handles – so long that even though the people could reach into the pot, the spoons were longer than the people's arms. They couldn't get food into their mouths. The rabbi couldn't believe how badly the people were suffering.

Then God said, "Now I will show you heaven."

They walked into a room that was identical to the first. Same big, round table, same pot of wonderful-smelling stew, same spoons with handles longer than the people's arms. But there was no screaming. The rabbi could hear the sounds of satisfied eating. These people were happy and well fed. God, seeing the rabbi's confusion, said, "It's simple, but it requires a specific skill. They have learned how to feed each other."

Chapter 7

START SOMEWHERE

When you're looking at a list of thousands of homes that are unsafe to inhabit, but you know people are living in them, and you have a limited amount of time with a limited amount of resources, you know at least two things: One, you're not going to fix all of these homes. Two, you have to start somewhere.

That's the dilemma George Sisler faced in Indianapolis. He's the executive director of a volunteer mobilization organization called One Heart – Many Hands, mentioned in chapter three. He had close to 2,000 volunteers ready to descend on the city. Some of the volunteers had very specific skills in home repair, construction, plumbing, electrical, etc. Most did not.

The city of Indianapolis identified tens of thousands of homes that had safety code violations, or orders for repairs. That meant many more thousands of people were living in unsafe conditions. Many of us would look at a list like this and shake our heads, thinking, "This problem is too big and I have too few people to tackle them and too little time."

Instead, George got to work. He tried to match volunteers and their abilities with homes that could use those abilities.

"There's always that one home," he said.

He came across a dwelling that had been used as a crack house and was in such disrepair from neglect and abuse that the city had condemned it. But a woman by the name of Freedom and her mother had moved in anyway, despite the boarded up windows and doors. They had never owned a home before. The city told George that it would take a minimum of $60,000 to make the house inhabitable, and that was if a contractor would even agree to do the work.

That's all George needed to hear. A team was willing to come in and start with Freedom's house, and within two weeks, the house was up to code and safe to live in.

For about a week, George and 1,600 volunteers from around the country and 200 volunteers from local Home Depot stores tackled 130 projects identified by the city as unsafe and in violation of city codes.

One Heart – Many Hands didn't repair all of the homes in Indianapolis, but they did a lot. They started with the first one.

He organized a similar effort in Orlando, Florida, a few years before. That "one home" that looked too complicated belonged to a man who had been in a car accident and was confined to a wheelchair. The house was falling apart, literally, and was excruciatingly difficult for the homeowner to move around inside. Volunteers widened the doorways so that the owner could pass through in his wheelchair, made the bathroom more accessible, repaired the hanging gutters and the collapsing fence, and made it possible for the man to live more easily in his own home.

Other volunteers worked with the city of Orlando to identify other code violations and disrepair, and fixed hundreds of houses.

"We went to the city and asked where we could be most useful to them," George said. "They saw that what they had estimated would take $25,000 to repair ended up costing about $2,500 because we were working with volunteers. Local stores saw what we were doing and donated supplies and sometimes even employees. The city saw us as an asset."

So did the homeowners.

Some of the homes in Orlando had significant mold problems. Sisler and his volunteers didn't have the ability to remove the mold, so he went to the local painter's union and described the situation. Union members immediately responded and donated their services.

"It's not that the union workers fell into our laps," George said. "We had to go to Orlando first and then figure it out."

George and the volunteers know that they aren't going to fix every home in a city where they are working. There are just too many problem homes. There are just too many problems.

"But we made a dent," he said.

What George has learned through his efforts to serve others is that if you look at the enormity of the problem, you will get paralyzed by how little you'll be able to accomplish in the grand scheme of things. George knew that his efforts in Indianapolis and in Orlando were not going to solve the problems of inadequate housing in those cities. At best, he was going to help a few hundred.

Likewise, when Gary and Steve went into Haiti after the earthquake, they knew they were not going to solve the country's problems of poverty and inequality and suffering.

But they knew they could do *something*. They knew they could start *somewhere*.

We can *all* start *somewhere*.

George is setting his sights a little higher now. Instead of cities, he's thinking countries. Cuba, in fact. As he did in Indianapolis, Orlando, New Orleans and elsewhere, he first went to the government agencies, churches and the people themselves and asked what they needed. He didn't presume to know. His experience has taught him that when the people in need are asked for their priorities, they are much more willing to open doors for the volunteers. But it's more than just efficiency. It's also a courtesy that acknowledges how groups work better when they work together. George arranged a meeting with Cuba's minister of health, and told him how volunteer efforts could help improve health care in that country. Then he asked the minister of health what the country needed.

The reception George received wasn't as positive as he hoped.

"He told me that what Cuba's hospitals and clinics needed was product – medicines, supplies, equipment," George said. "Before he would allow volunteers to come to the country, he said 'Let's first see if you can deliver the product.'"

George worked with Heart to Heart and several health care organizations in the U.S. to fill a shipping container full of the supplies the minister listed, and sent it to Cuba.

"The minister of health was testing our capacity to deliver on what we say we will deliver," George said. "Once he trusts us, who knows what other doors will open? But product won't change a relationship. Only face to face contact can do that. I'm excited about what they can teach us, too."

For Cuba, sending volunteers, equipment and supplies was the first step. You have to start somewhere.

RUNNING FOR LIFE

Jadh Lyke is an attorney whose practice focuses on civil, contract and business law. Her practice can be, in her words, "very dry." To keep her mind and body active during these "dry" times, she runs. She competes in 5k, 10k, and half-marathon races, and even an occasional full marathon. Often the races are fundraisers for hospital foundations, breast cancer and Parkinson's disease research.

As a teenager she went with a group of Heart to Heart volunteers to Kolkata, India, and worked alongside Mother Teresa and the other Sisters who served the destitute of that impoverished city. She played with children, visited a leper colony, and carried in medical supplies. The trip affected her in that she was able to see how little one really needs in order to be happy and joyful. At a young age, she realized that whatever she had was enough, and that she could put Mother Teresa's words into action, to "Do small things with great love."

As an adult several years later, she went with a Heart to Heart group to Haiti after the earthquake.

"In Haiti I saw the most need that I've ever seen," she said. "Nothing compares to the suffering that I saw there."

It wasn't just the need that got her attention, though. It was the proximity.

"Haiti is so close to us. It's a 90-minute flight from Disney World," she said.

One month after her Haiti trip, she organized a race to raise money for medical care in Haiti. She went to the Heart to Heart office and told them what she wanted to do, and that she wanted some flyers, banners, information on Haiti and volunteering, and maybe a little financial help for putting on the race.

"They were glad I was motivated, but they said they couldn't help me at the time," she said. "I'm not sure what was so hard about what I was asking. You just put on your shoes, pay a registration fee and run."

The competitor in her did not accept that answer, however. She did the race for Heart to Heart's efforts in Haiti *without* the help of Heart to Heart. She paid for the city permits, publicity and banners herself, about $800. She calculated the length of the run to be the same distance as what most people in Haiti have to walk to get to a medical clinic, and she chose a trail for the run instead of a paved street so it would be even more similar to a Haitian path. More than 100 runners and fifty volunteers showed up (including some from the Heart to Heart office), and she raised more than $7,000 for Haiti.

Now she does the race each year, and Heart to Heart works as a co-sponsor.

Fortunately for Heart to Heart and the people of Haiti, she decided to start somewhere.

When she was in Haiti, she worked in a Heart to Heart medical clinic in the Belaire Church of the Nazarene in Port-au-Prince. The church created the clinic after the earthquake as an additional site for those needing medical attention. When the pastor of the church found out that Jaydh was an attorney, he immediately asked her to develop a seminar to teach people about law.

"The pastor was smart," she said. "He knew that the people there could use an attorney!"

When she finished the seminar, she designed certificates for the participants, commemorating their new knowledge. But even that presented a challenge.

"When I tried to print out forty certificates on the church's printer, it took hours," she said. "At home it would take seconds."

Soon after she returned to the U.S. she bought a laser printer and had a Heart to Heart volunteer deliver it to Haiti a few weeks later. If she hears that someone is headed to Haiti, she has them take along printer cartridges.

Jaydh saw the conditions of Haiti and knew she couldn't fix that country. But she knew she could do something. She knew she could start somewhere. For her, it started with lacing up her running shoes.

Both George and Jaydh have learned a principle about serving others that seems counter-intuitive at first. When the need is so great, one might ask, why even try? What good will it do? George knew that there would still be thousands of people living in unsafe conditions after he left Indianapolis, Orlando, or Havana. Jaydh knew that people in Haiti would still be suffering even after she raised money for them.

But *not* doing something was *not* okay. They could do *something*. They could start *somewhere*.

This is how Gary and Steve felt about their work in Haiti. Once they started watching news accounts of the devastation from the earthquake, *not* doing something was not an option.

Even the way Gary first got into Haiti after the earthquake was a matter of starting somewhere without knowing the outcome. In his case, starting somewhere meant first getting airborne. He knew he needed to get into the country as soon as possible, but everyone – including the U.S. military – told him that there was no way to fly directly into the Port-au-Prince airport. It had been badly damaged by the earthquake, so it couldn't accommodate many aircraft. The U.S. military had taken over the area, and was allowing a limited number of humanitarian flights. Gary had found a volunteer to fly him there in a small plane, but he was told that he'd have to land in the Dominican Republic, a country that is on the same island as Haiti, and then arrange a ride into Haiti. He had seen the news accounts where the border crossing was backed up for miles. It could take days to get into a place that was only 700 miles away from the U.S.

Then he had an idea. What if he and the pilot registered their flight path from Florida to the Dominican Republic, but, once in the air, requested a change so that they could land in Port-au-Prince?

"It was worth a try, so the pilot agreed," Gary said. "We didn't have a plan, but we had a plane."

As they approached Haiti, the pilot contacted the Port-au-Prince control tower and said he had a U.S. Army Reserve colonel who was a medical doctor on board, and requested permission to land. Permission was granted.

Once he was on the ground and saw how vast the devastation was, Gary felt inadequate. He knew he had to start somewhere. He gave away the supplies he brought with him, and did whatever came next. Soon more volunteers arrived with more supplies. It was a small beginning that grew into

NOT OKAY

Some doctors, especially those with military ties like Gary, seem to be able to accomplish more than anyone else. They can organize convoys loaded with food and medicine. They can evacuate the neediest. They can evaluate situations, give orders, and move mountains. Not every volunteer is a doctor with military connections, but everyone can do something. Everyone can start somewhere.

In his book about slavery called *Bury the Chains*, Adam Hochschild tells of a man named Thomas Clarkson, who was about to finish his schooling in England in the late 1700s. As a requirement of graduation, Clarkson submitted his final essay, and the topic he chose was slavery, which was a part of everyday life at the time. Clarkson was embarking on his career as a priest in the Anglican Church, and as he traveled toward London by horse, he got to thinking about what he had written. The more he thought about slavery on that trip, the more it bothered him – the more wrong it seemed – and yet Clarkson couldn't think of what to do about it. Though he had written about it as a fact of life, it occurred to him that it was not acceptable to treat other human beings this way. What could he do? He got off the horse he had been riding. Clarkson sat down, troubled by the conclusions he was reaching.

"Here a thought came into my mind," he wrote later, "that if the contents of the Essay were true, it was time some person should see these calamities to their end."

That day, in 1785, was the beginning of the end of slavery.

For the next several years, Clarkson went from confidence to doubt regarding what he could do about the inhumanity he wrote about in his essay. He continued to question whether the issues he wrote about were true. Each time he would realize that yes, those things he wrote were true. And he would then think "Then surely some person should interfere," he thought.

"Only gradually, it seems," Hochschild wrote, "did it dawn on him that he was that person."[14]

Clarkson and others spent the next several decades in a campaign to end slavery. It started with a dissatisfaction of what he was confronting – that human beings were bought and sold like cattle. He knew he had to start somewhere.

EXCUSES, EXCUSES

There are at least three downsides to this thinking, though. Readers might think this chapter is saying drop everything, start a nonprofit, start a campaign, quit one's job, stop feeding one's family, and move to a developing country. Though some are called to do these things, (except maybe to stop feeding one's family) this is not a call to irresponsibility. It is, however, a call to becoming conscious of need all around us and that everyone has an opportunity to participate in relieving that need. They may not see massive results, but that isn't always the point. Everyone can do something. Everyone can start somewhere.

The second downside is that our efforts to serve others may not amount to much. They may not change anything. Many service groups have started over the years and fizzled soon after they began because of lack of funding, lack of organization and burnout by participants. Starting somewhere ended up in going nowhere.

And the third downside is that serving others can sometimes hurt more than help. In the book *Toxic Charity: How Churches and Charities Hurt Those They Help (And How to Reverse It)*, the author Robert Lupton writes:

"When we realize that we have the capacity (and responsibility) to meet a need, we naturally look for the most direct and immediate way to intervene," Lupton writes. "A homeless man is hungry, so we offer him food. A bright child is failing in school, so we help her with her homework. An aging widow's heat has been cut off, so we pay her gas bill. These are personal acts of compassion that address an immediate, correctable need."[15]

The problem, though, is that we realize there are more hungry people, smart kids and freezing old people. We feel as if we should increase our efforts to alleviate their conditions. We organize food drives, mentoring programs, adult adoption campaigns, get more people involved and open community centers. According to Lupton, these do little to help people meet their own needs and solve their own problems. They can sometimes do more harm than good, he says.

"They are entry points, but not ending points," he writes.[16] Eventually, those initial acts of service can grow into means by which the quality of people's lives can improve.

"Charity originates in the heart. It flows out to touch a hurting world. Compassion is the reflection of the divine, the in-person reassurance that there is care in our universe. But ... charity can be either toxic or transformative. To be ultimately redemptive, it must be carefully considered. Rushing in to rescue victims from calamity may be the very highest and noblest of acts. Partnering and investing with those entrapped in chronic need is an equally noble response. Wisdom is required to determine which is the more appropriate course in each particular case."[17]

"Starting somewhere" is a crucial part of serving others and improving the world. But as Lupton points out, unless that "somewhere" also leads to a relationship with those being served, not only is the improvement going to be short-lived, but marvelous opportunity will also be lost.

"Service seeks a need, a problem to fix, an object to pity," he writes. "But pity diminishes and respect emerges when servers find surprising strengths among the served, strengths not initially apparent when the served are seen as the nameless, needy poor. Perceptions change when servers discover unseen capacities, like the amazing ingenuity required to survive in harsh environments, or the deep faith that depends upon God for daily bread, or the sense of community that sacrificially shares meager resources so that those most vulnerable can survive. Authentic relationships with those in need have a way of correcting the we-will-rescue-you mind-set and replacing it with mutual admiration and respect." [18]

Lupton tells of a relationship that developed between a group of suburban church volunteers in Atlanta and those in the community whom the volunteers were serving food. The volunteers came on Wednesdays at noon to serve the poor.

"As 'the poor' in the food line became people with names and familiar faces, as personal stories were exchanged, friendships began to develop," Lupton writes. "The served were eventually invited to help serve food and even assist with food preparation. Mutuality grew. New recipe ideas were explored. Culinary skills were exchanged. While sweating together in the kitchen, the lifelong dream of four of the 'recipient' women eventually surfaced – to have their own restaurant."[19]

That kind of dream could never be realized without others who had the resources, Lupton writes, and without those who decided to start somewhere. But those Wednesday "service times" became planning sessions. Experts in the field were consulted. A plan was drafted. Money began to come in. A bigger group of friends developed.

The result is an excellent restaurant on the south side of Atlanta.

When Jesus saw that the thousands of people around him were hungry, he told his disciples to give them something to eat. They didn't have enough. But they had to start somewhere. They started with what they had, and eventually everyone was fed.

In the book *Heart and Soul: Awakening Your Passion to Serve*, there is a story that still haunts Gary. He was visiting the main orphanage in Kolkata, which housed 500 children, from babies to school age. What caught his eye was a glass case with a large lock. The Sisters took children to the case to let them look in. The children put their noses against the glass and pointed to the inside, oohing and ahhing.

"I looked over the tops of their heads to see what could be so fascinating," Gary said. "Was there a pet in there? Some kind of museum display? What I saw broke my heart."

There were three stuffed animals in that case. They were locked inside because there were only three, for 500 children. Dividing them equally would mean each child would get a little tuft of worn dirty polyester fur. So in order for all the children to just see the animals, they remained out of touch, protected by glass.

FedEx again participated in this airlift, and they had sent some of their employees on an assessment trip, and they were bothered by the very thing that bothered Gary. They were so moved that, when they returned to their London offices, they told their fellow employees what they saw. They established a collection point for donated stuffed animals that would go to Kolkata on the next airlift.

When the FedEx cargo plane landed in Kolkata a few months later, in addition to medicines it was carrying 10,000 stuffed animals.

Every child in that orphanage got to choose one to keep as his or her own, and the other animals were shared with orphanages throughout India.

Everyone can start somewhere. Three stuffed animals locked in a case became 10,000 because some FedEx employees realized they could start somewhere.

Chapter 8

MAKE IT LAST

E rnesto Sirolli worked in a government aid program in his native country of Italy. The program was inspired by the Peace Corps in the United States, and groups were sent around the world to help and serve others. One project in particular still stands out in his mind. It was when the well-intentioned people of Italy decided to teach people of Zambia how to grow food. They brought seeds from Italy to grow tomatoes and zucchini, and were amazed at the lush, fertile valley that existed all the way down to the Zambezi River. They couldn't understand why the people of Zambia weren't growing crops there.

"We taught the local people how to grow Italian tomatoes and zucchini," Sirolli said in a TED talk. "And of course, the local people had absolutely no interest in doing that, so we paid them to come and work, and sometimes they would show up. But instead of asking them how come they were not growing anything, we simply said 'Thank God we're here – just in the nick of time to save the Zambian people from starvation.'"

123

Everything grew beautifully. The tomatoes were bigger in this marvelous land than anything in Italy. Then, when the tomatoes were huge, red and ripe, about 200 hippos came up out of the river and ate them all.

The workers said to the Zambians, "My God! The hippos!"

The Zambians said "Yes, that's why we have no agriculture here."

"Why didn't you tell us?" the workers asked.

"You never asked," the Zambians said.

Sirolli said that he wondered if it was just the Italians who were blundering in Africa, but he saw that the Americans, the French, the English, were all making the same mistakes.

"I became quite proud of our project in Zambia, because, you see, at least we fed the hippos," he said.

The lesson?

"If you arrive in a community with arrogance and you don't listen to the local people, you don't ask, you are going to have your pride chewed off by the local hippos," he said.[20]

In the book *Toxic Charity: How Churches and Charities Hurt Those They Help (And How to Reverse It)*, Robert Lupton echoes Sirolli's point.

"Governments can give millions, rock bands can do benefit concerts, ex-presidents can champion causes, and churches can mobilize their volunteers," he writes. "But in the end what takes place in the community, on the street, in the home, is what will ultimately determine the sustainability of any development."[21]

Lupton's call is for "a progression from spontaneous acts of compassion to thoughtful paths to development." [22]

In contrast, the book *When Helping Hurts* tells of three people who moved into a high-crime area of Baltimore in an effort to serve the community. They didn't go into the community to save it, fix it, change it or give it a "blueprint." They went into the neighborhood to "live on the terms set by our neighbors," they said. They lived in this community for more than two years, had people to their home, and had picnics in parks, celebrated holidays together. They also had conversations with neighbors and asked what could be done to improve their community. The biggest priority for the neighbors was improved housing, they said. So the three new neighbors formed a chapter of Habitat for Humanity, with no money and no construction experience. This was a strategy that would "enable the people of the community – who had always been left out of the process and the benefits of urban development – to own, manage and be stewards of their architectural and economic environments," one of them said.

Four years after the three moved into the neighborhood, they built their first house. That doesn't sound very efficient, does it? Couldn't professional developers have done it faster and with more efficiency?

It depends on the goal.

For the three people who moved into the neighborhood in Baltimore, they said the goal was a process, not a product.

Their goal was to build "people, leaders, community, an economic base, and capacity, not a product for profit," they said. Those three no longer live in that neighborhood, but it is thriving under the leadership of people from that community. It has redeveloped a fifteen-block area where more than 200 homes have been renovated and made livable again. The community agency employs more than eighty people and runs programs for housing, employment, education, health care and the arts on a multi-million dollar budget. All of this from three people moving in, participating in the lives of those in the neighborhood, asking "what do you need?"[23]

BLUEPRINT VS. PARTICIPATORY

In the book, the authors make a distinction between the ways many people view serving others: one is what they call a "blueprint approach," and the other is called a "participatory approach."

The blueprint approach implicitly communicates, "I, the outsider, am superior; you are inferior; I am here to fix you." A participatory approach, in contrast, asks the poor at each step in the process, "What do you think?" And then really values the answers that are given. The very fact that the question is being asked is a powerful statement that says, 'I believe you have value, knowledge, and insights. You know things about your situation that I do not know. Please share some of your insights with me. Let us learn together."[24]

The participatory approach has not been the common practice in how people typically respond to Haiti. Throughout its history it seems that other countries and non-government agencies have responded to Haiti's needs based on what the countries or organizations *think* Haiti needs. It has been the blueprint approach. Whether it's to help with an economic crisis, a hurricane or an earthquake, outsiders have rushed in to fix the problem. Most of these outside groups presumably had good intentions. But the result was not always positive. Sometimes the cure left the country with a different problem.

In a National Public Radio program, *This American Life*, a story about an American doctor working in Haiti illustrated the different approaches. The doctor wanted a baby to be seen by a pediatric orthopedic doctor, but that doctor was in a different part of town over horrendous roads, and the trip would be expensive. In the old days, the doctor said, a non-Haitian group would have had all of the medical facilities in the same place.

"It makes you understand why a lot of NGOs still operate in the old foreigners-in-charge way," he said. "It's efficient." The Haitian way, he pointed out, was "the opposite of efficient."

But, the doctor said, this is part of the price of community building.

"If you want Haitians to create and sustain their own institutions," the narrator said, "this is what it looks like – slow and sometimes cumbersome."

But the alternative wasn't very attractive, either. In the face of the dysfunction and inefficiency, he could have just told everyone what to do.

In that scenario, "What was required of me was to build a citadel to become a dictator... a benevolent dictatorship," he said. "I could be the cowboy to fix the problems that would bring efficiency, service and security. What's wrong with that? Why not become a benevolent dictator?"

People have asked that question in countries – especially in Haiti – for hundreds of years.

"The problem that I found is that model creates, in a way, a new slave plantation mentality where the slaves become dependent upon the slave masters," he said. And in the end, one reaps the fruit of slavery – discontent, anger, violence.

"The choice to then go to the other extreme to purposely work hard at not becoming a dictator for the sake of building community means that people are going to suffer, people are going to die, goods will not be provided, services will not be rendered. . . . That's a terrible choice."

Community building and sustainability take time, because developing relationships takes time.

"It drives Americans crazy," the doctor said. "We're a fix-it culture. It's the height of evil, probably, from an American culture point of view, to not fix a problem when it's right there to fix."[25]

Fixing an immediate problem quickly can sometimes cause unintended consequences. When the 2010 earthquake occurred, hundreds of medical relief teams poured into Haiti and began providing free health care. What could possibly be wrong with that? In this case the outcome was that the health care professionals already working in Haiti were suddenly without work. Why would a Haitian go to a Haitian doctor who would charge for the services when he or she could go to a relief agency and get treated for free? Helping Haiti was important in providing short-term solutions, but in the long term the help contributed to additional dependency on foreigners. Health care professionals lost their livelihood, their businesses, and their families became dependent on others.

Further evidence of the "blueprint" approach is the central market of Port-au-Prince. According to Amy Wilentz' book, *Farewell, Fred Voodoo*, the Iron Market that had been the hub of commercial activity since the late 1800s was a busy, noisy, fly-infested swarm of humanity. Shoppers haggled with vendors over fruit, vegetables, clothing, electronics, and meat that hung in the hot, humid air. The market was destroyed by the earthquake and a subsequent fire. A new, modern market was rebuilt by a foreign company. The new market featured bright lights, refrigerated meat counters, garbage bins and ceiling fans. But sales are slow there. It didn't catch on. In fact, other outdoor markets have evolved elsewhere in Port-au-Prince, and business is very good at those locations. Not so at the new blueprint market. The company assumed that its methods were desirable, because this newer kind of market was successful in other parts of the world. The company didn't involve Haitians in the decision to modernize the market. The company assumed it knew what was best.[26]

JUST ASK

There is a lesson in this about serving others. When we see people in need, we often respond in ways that we think are best. Our motives are right. But often the results aren't there because we left out an important component – we didn't ask the people what they needed.

We have to start there.

In the New Testament of the Bible, in the book of Matthew, there is a story where Jesus and his disciples are walking through the city of Jericho. A blind beggar is brought to them and, even though it was obvious that the man was blind, Jesus asks the man what he wants. The man says he wants to see, so Jesus gives him his sight. Jesus could tell he was blind and didn't really need to ask, but serving others isn't just about *us* doing something for *them*. Serving others engages those we are serving. The people we're serving aren't projects.

They're people. Even Jesus respected the blind man enough to ask first.

Many churches, schools, civic organizations and other groups send their members out regularly on what are called short-term missions or service projects. The idea behind them is that groups from developed countries go into areas that are struggling, and the groups sometimes presume to know what the community needs. The groups might build buildings, dig wells, paint walls, install windmills, and even bring tractors and plows. They feel good about themselves and about what they accomplished. But when they return to these areas a year or more later, they wonder why the buildings are empty, the wells unused, the windmills inoperative and the farm equipment rusted. Often it's because the communities where these acts of service occurred were never consulted as to what the communities actually needed or wanted. Sometimes, as in the case of the farm equipment, it's because the community had no access to fuel to keep the machines operating. When the tank of gas provided by the volunteers became empty, the equipment was pushed to the corner.

In Haiti, Heart to Heart asks people two basic questions: "What are you trying to accomplish?" and "How can we help?"

"More often than not, we are told that no one has ever asked those questions," said Steve, Heart to Heart's executive director in Haiti. "With all of the organizations working in this country, that's hard to believe."

Heart to Heart learned this long ago when they put out a request for donations to help victims of Hurricane Andrew in 1992. The organization asked for food, emergency supplies, and new or like-new clothing. Heart to Heart filled 47 train cars with needed supplies that were sent to Florida. But in addition to the much-needed food, clothing and emergency supplies, Heart to Heart received ice skates, ski equipment and heavy winter clothing.

"I couldn't believe that people used this as an opportunity to empty their garages and get rid of their junk," Gary said.

More recently, medical supply organizations donated sophisticated examination tables for use in remote communities in Haiti as health clinics were established. The clinics desperately needed exam tables, but the donated tables needed electricity to function. The communities that needed them didn't have electricity.

Asking what people need is a critical piece in the participatory approach. This is where true development happens.

"We all know that *relief* work is easier to do than *development* work," said Steve. "With relief work, the needs are evident: people are suffering, drowning, starving, infected, etc. Development work takes more time and money. And to do it well, it takes relationship."

As the authors of *When Helping Hurts* admit, there are at least three reasons why relief work is easier than development work. The first reason is that many people believe that a handout of a tangible item solves the problem. A hungry person asks for food and we give her food or money. Hunger is an immediate need that demands an immediate solution. But what happens when that person is hungry again?

A second reason relief work is easier than development work is that relief work is usually simpler. "It is much simpler to drop food out of airplanes or to ladle soup out of bowls than it is to develop long-lasting, time-consuming relationships with poor people, which may be emotionally exhausting," the authors say. That's true whether it's about people with needs in our neighborhoods or in other countries.

The third reason relief work is easier than development work is that it's easier to raise money for relief work. When the tsunami hits, money pours in. When the neighbor's house is broken into, a collection is taken. "'We fed a thousand people today' sounds better to donors than 'We hung out and developed relationships with a dozen people today,'" the authors say.[27]

Still, meeting the immediate needs is important. Gary once asked Mother Teresa about the criticisms she received for focusing primarily on meeting the poor's immediate needs in Kolkata. Gary said her response was simple and direct: "She told me, 'My job is to give them a fish today. Someone else can teach them how to fish,'" he said.

But the biggest difference between relief and development is that development response lasts far beyond the crisis. When an emphasis is put on development, the efforts are intentional and strategic, enough so that when the one providing the service moves on, the benefits remain. Development, in its truest form, is sustainable.

Serving others is not in itself sustainable, according to the book *Toxic Charity*. The author makes a distinction between "serving others" and "developing others." Serving others helps people in the short term, but developing others "maintains the long view and looks to enable others to do for themselves," he said. "Serving others improves conditions, but developing others improves capacity." [28]

Even some well-run service programs "do little to strengthen the community's capacity to address its own needs," the author said. "And often they can work at cross purposes with community development. They are entry points but not ending points." [29]

There's an old saying that you can't just keep pulling people out of the river – eventually you have to go upstream and find out what's been pushing them in. It's one thing to ease someone's suffering, to respond to the emergency, to relieve the pain in the short term. Heart To Heart has spent much of its time and resources in meeting immediate needs after an earthquake, tornado, hurricane, tsunami or other kind of disaster. But sometimes meeting the short-term needs isn't the only answer. There's also a role for us to look long-term to see if there is something that could be done that would have a longer-lasting impact.

MICRO AND MACRO WORLDS

We live in two worlds: a micro world, where we respond and react to our immediate surroundings, and a macro world, where we live amid systems and cultures and traditions and practices that affect those surroundings. The story of the Good Samaritan shows a man dealing with the micro world he lives in. He sees that a man has been beaten and robbed and left for dead. The Good Samaritan cleans the victim's wounds, takes him to an inn and pays for his care. That's a micro system story. The parable doesn't show the Samaritan setting up a medical clinic to help other victims, or addressing the issues that cause people to beat and rob travelers. Those are the more macro issues.

And since we live in both micro and macro worlds – immediate circumstances that have longer-term impacts and causes – paying attention to just one or the other is only part of the story of serving others.

When the founders of Heart to Heart first went to Russia in 1991, they had heard that there were severe shortages of supplies in Russian hospitals. There were stories of doctors using the same needles and scalpels on different patients, of hospitals running out of bandages and gauze and anesthetic, and of widespread need for basics that are abundant in most metropolitan hospitals in most countries. They were completely out of antibiotics.

Gary and the others saw the empty shelves. The answers seemed obvious. But he understood how important it was to ask the Russians what they needed. The needs were so great that Heart to Heart knew it would take major partnerships to give the Russians what they were asking for. Several members on that early team were Rotarians, so it was obvious that the project should start there. The momentum quickly grew beyond their local Olathe, Kansas, chapter and involved Rotary clubs throughout Kansas City and the entire region.

Gary, being a family physician, then met with his professional organization, the American Academy of Family Physicians (AAFP), and enlisted their help. Within months, volunteers from both organizations arrived in a massive airlift and delivered the supplies personally.

But it wasn't a "one and done" event. For the next twenty years, Heart to Heart and the AAFP, with support from the U.S. State Department, delivered hundreds of millions of dollars' worth of medicine to Russia and the former Soviet Republics. More importantly, this partnership sponsored numerous physician training programs in obstetrics, pediatrics and family medicine, resulting in the establishment of permanent resident training programs in several countries. This shows how both relief and development can work together.

In Cascade Pichon, the remote part of southeast Haiti we've mentioned earlier in this book, Heart to Heart was asked to visit and assess the needs of this mountainous area.

"What we discovered was that this was one of the neediest areas of the country," Steve said. "They lacked schools and health care. The illiteracy rate was 95 percent. Cholera was rampant. They didn't have latrines or safe drinking water."

To make matters worse, as was previously described, the area was almost impossible to reach. The existing road was too steep, too severe, and too rough for most vehicles to drive to it. Everything depended on getting a better road.

So he worked with local governments and Heart to Heart volunteers to improve the road. And now that there is at least a passable road and a school has been built, teachers have arrived. A community that had a 95 percent illiteracy rate is now getting educated. A community that has never had health care now has a permanent medical clinic.

Leaders of Bel Anse, the regional capital, also met with Steve to assess their community. Steve asked what they needed. They said one of their needs was to get their radio station running again so they could get basic health information out to the 78,000 people living in the surrounding isolated areas.

A donation made through Heart to Heart has the station broadcasting again, with regular programming on health and hygiene, and a plan for how to stay on the air long-term.

"I would have never thought of that on my own," Steve said. "They knew what they needed."

HONEST DISTRUST

Robis Pierre grew up in the southern region of Haiti. He has degrees from universities in both Belgium and Montreal, and he returned to Haiti to work in a government office that is supposed to coordinate the activities of all NGOs in his country. It is a nearly impossible task. One of the reasons is that NGOs typically work independently from the communities where they are working, he said.

"Most NGOs do things temporarily and then leave," he said. "After they leave, the situation is worse than before. More often than not, they don't consider the particular needs, habits, etc. of the communities where they are working. They are just coming to start something new. But if you don't have a bottom-up approach, it will go back to the beginning phase."

He developed a distrust for the motives and effectiveness of the NGOs in his country.

"We came to the conclusion that no country can become developed with the actions of those NGOs because they are short-term actions," he said. "When you are addressing emergencies and when it doesn't fit with the habits of the people, it can be very harmful. Only sustainable action can lead to development."

He was skeptical when he was introduced to Steve and Heart to Heart.

"I had suspicions because of the actions of other NGOs that I knew," he said. "But through our exchanges I have been able to have a vision of this long-term work that we need to do to create better development. I found a connection with the vision of the Haitian government to Dr. Weber's vision with Heart to Heart. I know it's important to help cure people, but it's more important to prevent them from being sick. To prevent sickness is to educate. To prevent sickness is to help people be responsible for themselves and for their community. You have to empower people so they know what to do."

Relief work is important and often necessary after a disaster or crisis. Getting from survivability to sustainability isn't easy. Going from short-term relief to long-term development takes time. It starts with asking the question. But the goal is not for outsiders to keep delivering services forever. It is for the local communities to address their own needs without outside assistance. When you do that, you make it last. The hippos have to look elsewhere for their dinner.

Chapter 9

TRANSFORM YOUR LIFE

E verything Steve Weber thought he knew about being a
missionary was tossed out during his first few weeks in
Haiti in the early 1970s. He had training in cross-cultural
ministry, knew some history about the country, and had
theological education that would help him provide the people
of Haiti a clearer picture of the nature of God.

Until he heard about the famine.

"It was something that absolutely did not fit into my world
view, my theology, nor my ability to understand," he said.

Soon after he arrived, he began hearing reports of starvation
occurring on La Gonave, an island about two hours by boat off
the coast of western Haiti. A drought had destroyed the crops,
and the desperate residents had eaten the seeds designated
for next year's growing season. Some of the people had
already died.

It was difficult to reach the areas that were hardest hit
because of the remoteness of the location. There were no roads

to speak of, so no relief agencies could bring in their relief supplies. Anyone able to leave the area migrated to the main island of Haiti. Those who remained were the elderly, the very young and the extremely poor. They all faced starvation.

Steve toured the area on horseback, and he saw dozens of people leave this world because the lack of nourishment kept them from being able to battle preventable diseases. People were susceptible to any number of illnesses that would typically not kill them. But without food. . . .

Steve had come to Haiti after being pastor of a church in Southern California where the people in his congregation – even the poor – had plenty to eat. That congregation might have been suffering from spiritual hunger, but it wasn't killing them.

"The church where I was pastor had enough resources within itself to stop this ridiculous, unnecessary suffering and loss of life," he said.

Once word spread that a section of Haiti was starving to death, food started arriving in the country by the tons from around the world. Hundreds of tons. And most of it sat in warehouses in Port-au-Prince. It was too difficult to get it to La Gonave. The people for whom the food had been donated were not seeing it. Steve called people from his denomination in the United States and asked for money. His contacts thought he wanted money for food.

"I told them I didn't need money for food," he said. "There was plenty of food. There was more food available than the people on the island could ever use."

Steve raised $20,000 with a few phone calls. He used the money to buy a truck, a boat, twenty donkeys and materials to build two food depots. People in local churches became volunteer donkey drivers, security guards, builders and food distributors. Before long they were feeding more than 18,000 children, providing care for hundreds of pregnant women, and building roads so that supplies could get to the remote areas more easily. The U.S. ambassador to Haiti gave Steve a special citation. His alma mater, California State University at Long Beach, named him alumnus of the year.

His original assignment, when he was sent by his church denomination to Haiti, was to be an administrator and teacher of an Introduction to Theology course. After this experience at La Gonave, he discarded most of his theology notes and started over. He reworked those notes, beginning with a different question from what many people would ask. After similar experiences, many people ask, How could a loving God allow this kind of suffering to happen? Instead of that question, Steve asked these two: How could good and godly people die of starvation when they live so close to a wealthy nation like the U.S.? More to the point: How could good and godly people *allow their neighbors* to die of starvation?

"Such a reality didn't make any sense to me," Steve said. "And it still doesn't, after all these years."

A dialogue between God and a person who witnesses suffering could go like this:

Man: "God, how could you allow this to happen?"

God: "Interesting question. I was going to ask you the same thing."

In the book *Mountains Beyond Mountains*, Paul Farmer translates a Haitian proverb this way: "God gives us humans everything we need to flourish, but he's not the one who's supposed to divvy up the loot. That charge was laid upon us."[30]

After this early experience in La Gonave, Steve was transformed.

"I never became much of a theologian, but what I did become was a person who is not able to stand by and see problems ignored when I know I can help," he said. "Often I can't do a lot, but I can do something. I have lived my entire life quite differently since that first encounter with starvation."

The "temporary" food program he started in La Gonave is still going strong after more than forty years. It became a permanent hot lunch program in hundreds of Haitian schools.

"VOLUNTEERING CHANGED ME"

When we serve others, something happens to us. Our focus changes. Our ego diminishes. We start to see the world through a prism other than, What can you do for me? We start to ask, What can I do for you? And when we start asking that question, everything changes. We are transformed.

In her book *Take This Bread*, author Sara Miles describes how she worked in a church in San Francisco that developed a feeding program for hungry people in the church's neighborhood. Many of those who came to receive free food ended up becoming volunteers in the program. She tells of Teddy, who came to the church while living on the street.

"I came here to get food, and then I thought I could volunteer, and volunteering changed me," Teddy said. "After all those years of being a drug addict, living on the streets, this gave me the sense that there was the possibility of happiness again. Now every time I give out food and make contact and am able to smile at somebody, even if I can't speak their language, I'm just really touched – I'm being fed by it."[31]

Teddy said that once he started serving others – even though his personal circumstances hadn't changed – he was able to see beauty in a way he hadn't experienced before.

"I used to walk by stuff and never see it," he said. "Now I feel myself connected to the rest of the universe. Giving people food, I can really feel I've done something worthwhile at the end of the day."[32]

Teddy's life was transformed when he began to serve others.

Janice Ballard's life changed after her first visit to Haiti. She was a graduate student at the University of Memphis, and needed to complete a practicum experience for her master's in public health degree. She had seen a documentary about Haiti, and talked to people about trying to connect with one of the major nongovernment organizations there. She wanted to study how NGOs respond to crisis. Then the 2010 earthquake occurred. Someone told her that the organization she should call was Heart to Heart. She thought that Heart to Heart could get her introduced to some of the larger groups.

"I called Gary Morsch and told him what I was interested in, and he was very enthusiastic," she said. "He told me to come to Haiti, and he'd introduce me around, so I did."

Ballard is from Guyana in South America and is comfortable in cross-cultural settings. She sat in on meetings with Heart to Heart staffers and board members and Haitian leaders who were treating the injured and sick and were planning for how to reach more people. After hearing how they talked about community health, sustainability, accountability, and empowering the local people, she felt like this was the NGO she wanted to study. But she did far more than study. She went to the Bel Aire clinic and saw how hundreds of people waited for hours every day to be seen by a doctor. It was a captive audience.

"I started talking with them about public health issues while they waited, and they were very interested," she said.

She taught them about hygiene and sanitation, cultural myths about how diseases are spread, the importance of following prescription orders for medicine, high blood pressure, diabetes, parasites and environmental hazards. She asked them questions and listened. She developed materials that could be taught by Haitians to Haitians, especially those who could not read or write. When she talked to Heart to Heart staffers about creating a curriculum for the Haitian people, the staffers asked how soon she could put it together.

"Every cell in my body came alive when they asked that," she said. "I knew what I was put on this earth to do."

She began visiting Haiti regularly, and expanded the number of places where she taught. The focus was on disease prevention. Since many of these areas have no access to health care at all, it made more sense to her to train people in how to avoid disease than in how to treat disease.

"In the more rural areas, where there is no health care at all, people depend on the voodoo priests for everything, especially for curing illness, so we invited the priests in for training," she said. "Now they're training their own people on these topics. They love being included."

Her focus on serving others shifted some aspects of her personal life.

"The comforts in life that I thought were so important – something like air conditioning, for instance – became of little value to me," she said. "I'm not the focus of my attention any more. As a result, it's like I'm 100 percent alive. When you serve others, you live beyond yourself."

She also noticed that some of the same issues she saw in Haiti were occurring in her home city of Memphis, issues such as high infant mortality, and preventable diseases. She now works in community health in Memphis, and she leads volunteer teams from the BD company to Haiti a few times a year.

"Everybody is searching for their purpose in life," she said. "But you see your purpose in serving others. It's like a magnet."

WILL THIS HELP?

Art Fillmore, the Vietnam War veteran who was mentioned in chapter four, by his own admission had no desire to see Vietnam in person, in a movie, or in a book. But his nightmares had bothered him for twenty-five years. When Gary invited him to accompany Heart to Heart on a humanitarian airlift to Vietnam, Art reluctantly accepted. This time he had a duffel bag full of medicine instead of weapons. On a tour of a hospital in the same region where Art had been involved in countless firefights, a doctor pointed out a young boy with a kidney disease. The boy's abdomen was swollen and he was in great pain. Art asked the doctor how they were treating the boy, and the doctor pointed to an array of herbal medicines.

Art started pulling out boxes from his duffel.

"Will anything in here help?" he asked.

The doctor saw a box of antibiotics and looked directly at the boy's father.

"Your boy is going to live," the doctor said.

This second Vietnam trip changed Art forever.

"Volunteers think they are giving a gift to those they are serving," Art said. "But the reality is that the act of volunteering is a gift back to the volunteer. It changes you in some mysterious way."

When left to ourselves, we often think only of what we need, want, or aspire to do. That kind of living is, quite frankly, boring. Adding "others" to our lives is a transformational act.

"Serving others changes you," said George Sisler, of One Heart – Many Hands. "You think you are going somewhere to help someone, and you are. But in the meantime, you become a different person. A better person."

Beth Crocker was a college student preparing for a career in biological research when she went with Heart to Heart to Guatemala to help install water filters in villages that had nearly been destroyed by mudslides after heavy rains. She had been to Guatemala before as a child because she has family there. But she saw a different side of Guatemala this time.

"This really awakened me and made me want to do something now," she said. "Doing research, being behind the scenes is important, but this experience made me want to do more than that."

She changed her major to nursing, and began volunteering in urban medical clinics in Kansas City.

"The community you serve can be overseas or in the city where you live," she said.

Dylan Aebersold, the student in chapter three who helped his college raise money to build a school in Haiti, said that before he volunteered, he had his life planned out.

"My second day in Haiti I was a different person," he said. "I was saying to myself, what do I have to do to get back here? It even changes how you see where you live. I see things locally where I can serve, and I never saw them before."

This was Jon North's experience, too, after going on humanitarian service trips to Guyana, Costa Rica, and Los Angeles as a college student.

"These volunteer experiences put your own life into perspective," he said. "The things I struggled with back home were nothing compared to what most of the world struggles with. We truly are kings in our first-world culture. After a few experiences I decided I wanted to give the rest of my life to working for others."

North started working for Heart to Heart in its second year of existence and eventually became its CEO.

The earthquake altered Delson Merisier's focus, too, but in a different way. Merisier is a prominent OB/GYN doctor in the Leogane area of Haiti, and the disaster rattled more than just his clinic and home. It made him take stock of what he was doing with his life. Just as he finished delivering a baby on January 12, 2010, the ground beneath him shook and he saw the two-story school next to his clinic collapse. Then the second floor of his clinic crumbled into the first floor. For twenty minutes the earthquake and the aftershocks took down building after building, including his beautiful new home, right before his eyes.

By the next morning, the twelve-mile highway from Leogane to Port-au-Prince was impossible to drive on, not because of the major cracks in the pavement, but because it had become the nation's morgue. Bodies were placed on the highway by the thousands – there was nowhere else to place them.

Merisier's family survived, but they lost their homes and medical clinic. Their new home was a tent on top of his clinic's rubble. The NGOs that came in to help Haiti provided medical care for free, which made his medical practice even more damaged, since being a doctor was how he made his living. When he met people from Heart to Heart, he realized what had been missing in his professional life before the earthquake.

"My former partnerships had been based upon professional connections first, and everything else came after," he said. "But with Heart to Heart there developed first a deepening friendship and growing trust. I began to realize that friendship and trust were even more important than the professional aspects of the relationship."

Merisier is building his home again, repairing his clinic, and is now head of Leogane's Health Department. He lost all of his material possessions, and he was tempted to leave the area for greater material reward, but he realized that "Haiti needs me now more than ever," he said. "Money is not everything. I must utilize my skills to help my people."

GIVE IT BACK

One of the reasons we resist being transformed is that we simply can't imagine the possibility. In many cultures, young people are instructed to plan their lives out and do whatever it takes to stick to that plan. When everything is carefully prescribed, there isn't much room for imagination, or surprise.

When Gary talks to college students, he tells them the opposite of what most career counselors advise. Instead of telling students to list their goals and dreams, he says to do the opposite.

"If someone gives you a blank piece of paper and says, 'Write down what you want to do with your life,' give the paper back," he says. "If I would have done that I would have said that I wanted to be a doctor, see lots of patients and play golf on Wednesdays. Leave your life open-ended. The poet Rilke says to 'live the questions.' Life is greater and more interesting than you can imagine, so don't limit yourself to your own imagination. It's going to be much bigger, if you're open."

The poet Rainer Maria Rilke said that there are great discoveries waiting to be made when we take risks of discomfort.

"Why do you want to shut out of your life any uneasiness, any miseries, or any depressions?" Rilke wrote in the book *Letters to a Young Poet*. "For after all, you do not know what work these conditions are doing inside you."[33]

Serving others isn't just for individuals, though. Sometimes the practice of serving others can transform an entire organization. That's what BD discovered when its employees started volunteering in different parts of the world. Vince Forlenza, the CEO, saw a difference in his company when, after providing low cost products for vaccinations to the World Health Organization, employees went to some of those areas to volunteer and see the impact of their products.

"It was important to us to have those employees come back and share those experiences with their colleagues," he said. "One of the purposes of our company is to help eliminate unnecessary suffering and death, so it's important for us to combine the purpose of our company with the experiences of our people. Our company is interested in both product development and people development."

BD volunteers have been in several countries in Africa, after some toured regions on that continent to see the devastation of HIV and AIDS. The enthusiasm for volunteering caught on quickly in the company and became part of the corporate culture. After the earthquake in Haiti, the company looked for an organization with whom they could connect right away. They found Heart to Heart.

"Working with Heart to Heart is almost too easy because the whole organization is involved around volunteerism," said Jenn Farrington, BD's director of social investing. "Heart to Heart had needs, and we had people who could help."

BD volunteers work with direct care treatment in remote areas. They provide education for local health care workers, train lab technicians, and do construction for clinics.

In addition to providing medical products in Haiti through Heart to Heart, BD has donated equipment to Partners in Health and to the Centers for Disease Control and Prevention.

"The only reason we were able to work with those other organizations is that Heart to Heart helped us navigate in the country," Farrington said.

Forlenza, the CEO, said that BD and Heart to Heart had complementary sets of skills that made the connection easy.

"They knew the country, knew the actors, knew the history, had continuity and understanding of the situation, and they do everything very efficiently," he said. "Our employees go to Haiti to volunteer and they come back seeing the immediate impact of their efforts. They see that their efforts matter. Then they come back to the company and talk about it. Their experience reinforces the good things we're doing in our company."

Simply put, serving others gives life its meaning. How we treat others not only affects others' lives, but it also affects ours. This is how we become more interesting, fruitful characters in our own life's story. It's how we change for the better.

THE CURE

But it's not easy. It's easier to *not* be transformed. It's easier to stay just the way we are.

It may be easier, but very few of us really *want* to stay just the way we are.

In a commencement speech at Syracuse University, the writer George Saunders said that deep down inside, most of us want to live more meaningful lives.

Saunders said we are all built with some confusions that go far back into our evolutionary development. The first confusion is that we believe we are central to the universe, and that our story is the *only* story. The second is that we're separate from everyone else. There's us, and there's the rest of the world. The third is that we're permanent fixtures on earth. We'll be here forever. There is tension, though, with these built-in confusions and with what we actually want, Saunders said.

"What we really want, in our hearts, is to be less selfish," he says, "more aware of what's actually happening in the present moment, more open, and more loving."

Eventually, most of us see how illogical it is to remain selfish, he says. We realize that we aren't the central point of the universe, that other people's acts of kindness toward us have helped change us, that our own sense of importance diminishes as we see the bigger world. And as these changes occur, we see another one occurring – that we become more loving.

So if we are going to become kinder and more loving eventually anyway, Saunders' advice is to "Hurry up. Speed it along. Start right now. There's a confusion in each of us, a sickness, really: selfishness. But there is also a cure."[34]

Serving others – showing kindness – being more loving to the person who has lost a child in an earthquake, or a home in a tornado, or a job, or, fill in the blank, changes you.

It changed Ed Overholt, one of the doctors mentioned in previous chapters who volunteers with Heart to Heart. Ed performed heart surgery on a little boy in China that saved the boy's life. The importance of the operation was obvious to Ed at a personal level. Both of his sons needed to be resuscitated when they were young.

"Any parent who gets their child back after such an event knows how lucky I felt to help a team dedicated to passing this gift on to other parents," Ed said.

During the procedure, the child's parents, a simple farming couple from the area, waited outside. After the surgery, Ed went out and told them their only son was doing well and the procedure was a success. They thanked him profusely and then through an interpreter asked for a piece of tissue paper on which they wrote their address and asked Ed to write his address on a second one. They said they wanted to send a note of thanks and then said something Ed said he would never forget. They said they would tell their son when he was a man about the American doctor who cared enough to come and help his heart when he was a little boy. "They wanted him to thank me as well when he was grown and understood," Ed said.

Two years later, Ed was back in the same region in China for another volunteer visit with Heart to Heart. He saw this child and his family again. The boy was healthy, and Ed encouraged the family with his bright outlook. The father reminded Ed that he hoped his son would be able to personally thank Ed when the boy became a man.

"I assured him that I had all the thanks I needed," Ed said. "Driving away from the hospital, it struck me that I likely would never see them again. Yet a small act had connected us forever. It changed them and it changed me. The effects of our acts of service to each other performed in a few hours or a few days can last a lifetime. We only have to be willing to take the first step and allow ourselves to be used."

The experience reminded Ed of what he believes is our purpose on earth.

"It is to follow the Golden Rule Christ taught: to treat others out of our resources of time or talent or money as we would be treated," he said. "Buddhist or Christian, Chinese or American, we are brothers and here to give love from one heart to another."

This isn't something we do from a script. Opportunities present themselves, and we respond to them or not. When we do, we are changed forever.

"If the point of life is the same as the point of a story, the point of life is character transformation," said Donald Miller in his book *A Million Miles in a Thousand Years*. In most short stories, novels, movies or nonfiction narratives, the main character changes in some way – the protagonist is transformed. "He's a jerk at the beginning and nice at the end, or a coward at the beginning and brave at the end," Miller said. "If the character doesn't change, the story hasn't happened yet. And if story is derived from real life, if story is just condensed version of life, then life itself may be designed to change us so that we evolve from one kind of person to another."[35]

How can we live transformed lives? Rick Warren, the pastor of Saddleback Church in Southern California, and author of *The Purpose Driven Life*, sums it up this way: We have three choices in how to live.

You can *waste* your life. We all know people (and some of us *are* those people) whose gifts, resources and abilities are all collecting dust in the garage. Maybe through neglect, maybe even abuse, the purpose for which some people are living is squandered.

You can *spend* your life. We also know people who think of themselves as the center of the universe, and use their gifts and resources exclusively on themselves, to satisfy their own desires. The appetite for satisfying the self never stops growing.

Or you can *invest* your life. The way we invest our lives, so that there is continuous meaning, is by serving others.

Occasionally, Gary is asked to give commencement speeches at medical schools. He finished one speech at the

University of Oklahoma's medical school (his alma mater) this way.

"The most powerful tool you have is not your stethoscope, or the array of lab tests and MRI's and everything else you have at your disposal," he told the future physicians. "The most powerful tools you have are your heart, your spirit, your soul, your care, your love, your compassion. The greatest impact you make on your patients will not come from your great abilities or knowledge or technical skills, but from your heart.

"The greatest power in the world is the power of serving others."

About

HEART TO HEART INTERNATIONAL

Heart to Heart International (HHI) is a non-profit, 501(c)(3), non-governmental (NGO) humanitarian relief organization that is first and foremost a volunteer-based movement focused on engaging ordinary people in meaningful service. Founded on Christian principles in 1992, HHI continues to execute its fundamental mission motivated by the belief that everyone has something to offer those in need. HHI invites all people to serve the poor, the hurting and those in need of all nations –with their time, talent and resources.

This emphasis on volunteerism has been intentionally integrated into programs with the goal of volunteers having a transformative, life-altering experience. The goal is to ignite a spark of compassion and purpose forever changing the way our volunteers view people in need and their role in responding to that need – based on the faith-based principle of putting your faith into radical action. By touching the lives of millions of people, HHI volunteers are infected with what is referred to as the "the ripple effect" – their multiplied impact is changing the world far beyond the walls of Heart to Heart International.

This is most evident in the work HHI carries out in the face of natural disasters – supplying medical supplies, pharmaceuticals, equipment and medical teams of doctors, P.A.s, nurses and willing volunteers. Since 1992, more than $1 billion of aid and supplies has been delivered to over 150 countries, including the United States. HHI responds to both domestic and international disasters, but the organization also supplies volunteers with resources to improve their local communities with supplies for building and renovation projects for homes and schools. With the support of volunteers from corporate, civic and religious groups, and universities, communities are also able to offer healthcare clinics in inner city areas – free health fairs, screenings and training – not just in the United States, but around the world.

Annually, HHI assists 250 organizations with over $100 million in humanitarian aid and supplies. This level of assistance has created strong partnerships with major Fortune 500 companies and the largest pharmaceutical companies in the world. Named to Forbes magazine's prestigious list of "America's 200 Largest Charities," HHI is also recognized as one of the leaders in donor efficiency and charitable commitment. More than 98% of all contributions go directly to relief and development programs – all administrative and fundraising activities are supported by less than 2% of their total contributions.

As HHI has become one of the premier volunteer deploying organizations in the country, it has developed a sterling reputation for quality disaster response and humanitarian programs, particularly in Haiti.

Helping to meet the needs of victims of natural disasters, or of economic downfall, while seeing volunteers find a renewed sense of purpose in their own lives and workplace is the transformational difference Heart to Heart hopes to accomplish with anyone willing to partner with them.

HISTORY

At the close of the Cold War, Dr. Gary Morsch, a family physician from Olathe, Kansas, traveled with several other medical professionals to Russia to assess the state of patient care in the Soviet Union. The group witnessed a healthcare system on the brink of collapse. Motivated by what he saw, Dr. Morsch challenged his local Rotary Club to help provide medicines and medical supplies to hospitals in Moscow. He had toured several first-rate facilities and met many talented physicians. But their pharmacies were empty, and they had no way of providing patients with life-saving medicines.

Local collection drives soon spread. Major pharmaceutical companies joined the effort by donating much-needed products. Even the U.S. government got involved by providing the largest Air Force cargo plane in its fleet to fly the medical aid to Russia. On May 22, 1992, the C-5A Galaxy aircraft landed in Moscow. The aid was distributed to 15 area hospitals, and patients began receiving the care they needed.

A gift from the heart of America to the heart of Russia— the Heart to Heart Airlift—became a reality because hundreds of volunteers and caring corporate partners joined together to help people in need. At the time, it was the largest volunteer airlift in U.S. history.

The spirit behind that first project is still alive and well at Heart to Heart International today. As it works to create healthier communities around the world, the organization is motivated by the same principles that guided that first group of visionaries:

Help people in need. Heart to Heart International helps millions of people each year through humanitarian initiatives that improve health in underserved communities across America and around the world.

Do it efficiently. Because of donor generosity, Heart to Heart International is able to operate with a low overhead of less than two percent—meaning more than 98 percent of every contribution goes directly to humanitarian programs.

Let everyone serve. Heart to Heart International was founded on the belief that everyone has something to offer to those in need and can participate in humanitarian mission.

Make it transformational. The organization wants volunteers to find a renewed sense of purpose in their lives.

HOW YOU CAN GET INVOLVED

Visit our website at

www.hearttoheart.org

and find a place to serve!

Or contact Heart to Heart at:

Heart to Heart International

13250 West 98th Street

Lenexa, KS 66215

Phone: 913.764.5200

END NOTES

1 Paul Farmer, *To Repair the World* (Berkeley: University of California Press, 2013), 98.

2 Anne Lamott, *Plan B* (New York: Riverhead Books, 2005), 307-8.

3 Frederick Buechner, *Wishful Thinking* (New York: HarperOne, 1993), 95.

4 Amy Wilentz, *Farewell, Fred Voodoo* (New York: Simon & Schuster, 2013), 81.

5 Ibid., 81.

6 Ibid., 197.

7 Ibid., 16.

8 YouTube. "We Came Over to Sit." Online video clip. *YouTube,* 10 April, 2010. Web. 25, October 2014.

9 Paul Rogat Loeb, *The Impossible Will Take a Little While* (New York: Basic Books, 2004), 192.

10 Mark Schuller, *Killing With Kindness* (New Brunswick: Rutgers University Press, 2012), xi.

11 Paul Farmer, *Haiti After the Earthquake* (New York: PublicAffairs Books, 2011), 332.

12 Farmer, *To Repair the World*, 64-65.

13 Ibid., 65.

14 Ibid., 24-25.

15 Robert D. Lupton, *Toxic Charity* (New York: HarperOne, 2011), 197.

16 Ibid., 168.

17 Ibid., 188-189.

18 Ibid., 190.

19 Ibid., 190-191.

20 YouTube. "Want to Help Someone? Shut Up and Listen." Online video clip. *YouTube,* 26 November, 2012. Web. 25, October 2014.

21 Lupton, *Toxic Charity*, 85.

22 Ibid., 189.

23 Steve Corbett and Brian Fikkert, *When Helping Hurts* (Chicago: Moody Publishers, 2012), 77-79.

24 Ibid., 137.

25 This American Life, "Compound Fracture" (WBEZ), http://www.thisamericanlife.org/radio-archives/episode/408/island-time?act=2 (Accessed October 25, 2014).

26 Wilentz, *Farewell Fred Voodoo*, 274-277.

27 Corbett and Fikkert, *When Helping Hurts,* 114.

28 Lupton, *Toxic Charity*, 167.

29 Ibid., 168.

30 Tracy Kidder, *Mountains Beyond Mountains* (New York: Random House, 2004), 79.

31 Sara Miles, *Take This Bread* (New York: Ballantine Books, 2008), 215.

32 Ibid., 216.

33 Rainer Maria Rilke, *Letters to a Young Poet*, (New York: MJF Books, 2000), 80.

34 Lovell, Joel. "George Saunders's Advice to Graduate." *New York Times*. N.p., 31 July 2013. Web. 25 Oct. 2014.

35 Donald Miller, *A Million Miles in a Thousand Years* (Nashville: Thomas Nelson, 2009), 68.